MOBILE COMMERCE 3.0

T0125127

www.royalcollins.com

MOBILE
COMMERCE

3.0

(Revised Edition)

JIANG RUXIANG

Books Beyond Boundaries

ROYAL COLLINS

Mobile Commerce 3.0 (Revised Edition)

Jiang Ruxiang

Published in 2022 by Royal Collins Publishing Group Inc.
Groupe Publication Royal Collins Inc.
BKM Royalcollins Publishers Private Limited

Headquarters: 550-555 boul. René-Lévesque O Montréal (Québec) H2Z1B1 Canada
India office: 805 Hemkunt House, 8th Floor, Rajendra Place, New Delhi 110 008

Original Edition © CITIC Press Group

ISBN: 978-1-4878-0939-3

To find out more about our publications, please visit www.royalcollins.com.

CONTENTS

CONTENTS

E-COMMERCE: A BUSINESS

In the past, reading was an expensive hobby, and required visits to a library. Today, when switching on one's mobile phone, an abundance of books and e-books are available for free.

People previously read newspapers to access news and learn about the world. Today, everyone with a mobile phone is plugged into the media, taking part in the spread of news and information.

In the past, earning money required heavy investments, making expensive payments in expensive shops, and spending money on labour and advertising. Today, however, one need not spend money, but spend time on phone exchanges and interactions. This transforms people from simple consumers to consumer businesses – which I call the "we-channel". We have come into an age referred to as the "Mobile Internet Era", in which the battle of business occurs at our fingertips. This is an era in which the consumer can be an active participant in every transaction.

In the "Cloud World" of the Internet, entrepreneurship does not rely on capital but on people. The "Cloud" destroys the hardware threshold set by the rich, allowing ordinary people to start businesses with ease. Rather than money, one needs only wisdom, bravery and action. This is equilibrium. In the world of the mobile Internet, when the wealthy are at a loss they may finally perceive the truth: when birds fly, gold on their backs is not an asset, but a burden.

As such, in the mobile Internet world, people are the only true asset. As a result of the market, Amazon is fearful of Facebook in the US, while Alibaba is intimidated by WeChat in China. This is because the majority of people use online shopping marketplaces once or twice a week, yet use social media on a daily basis. Amazon and Taobao operate plainly for business purposes, while Facebook and WeChat revolve around life. Life is certainly greater than business.

But, what is it that Facebook and WeChat really do? Put simply, these sites broaden interpersonal relationships via mobile phones, extending previously offline "household affairs" to the online world. As a result, long separated schoolmates and friends may be reunited, loved ones gathered together; a "group" can become an "organisation".

Mobile Internet-based social platforms are shaking the gates of almost all industries. People gather in online masses, intimidating the powerful bank magnates, telecom operators and retail tycoons who were once in power. In the past, who did these giants ever have to fear?

When comparing the ideologies of the mobile Internet and traditional industry, it is like imagining a battle between nuclear weapons and basic rifles. Today, essential change has taken place in the relationship between the user and the product. You may recall the famous saying: "I love you, but it's none of your business."

Indeed, it is true that people do not truly love products, but their own desire to consume. Human happiness occurs within defined circles: others are part of my circle just as I am part of the circles of others. In an age where everyone sees themselves at the center of their own circle, it is actually as if there are no centers at all. Instead, everyone has become a part of a much greater interpersonal network. In such an open world of human interconnection, where do control and power lie?

With large traditional enterprises still obsessed with economic scale, with the brainwashing of users and the power of authority and organisations, individual power is growing wildly – a weed that will engulf the whole business world.

It is a grand banquet for mortals rather than gods, a battle for "people" rather than resources, which I call "UBER Talent", a marathon of "sharing" that will destroy the past and unite consumers, manufacturers and service providers.

Of course, you may ask, is this not an exaggeration?

In fact, this is no exaggeration, as the tribe-like circles engendered by mobile phones transcend space and time, like the source of a strong wind. In the course of history, it is indeed human nature that stands as victor.

———.———

CHAPTER 1

THE DATA AGE: A NEW "WORLD WAR"

At noon EST on the 9th of June, 2015, Jack Ma was invited to make a speech for nearly a thousand business leaders at the famous New York Economic Club, in which he remarked, "In this era of the Internet and Data Technology (DT), I think a new business platform has been born. The 'Third World War' is on its way. This will not be a war between countries, but one that takes on disease, poverty and climate change. I think this is the inevitable future of mankind. All nations, all countries, must be united. It is up to the younger generation, not weapons, relying on computers and mass data to solve human, social problems."

Jack Ma elevated "DT" as part of a world war, to be directed at tackling the major issues facing humankind. This technological development is an indication of strength, posing a competition between countries: whoever can establish a competitive edge in the "DT Era" stands to win over a new century.

DT is not the Internet – it is "Internet+"

A major upgrade has taken place, from the Internet to "Internet+". According to Jack Ma, this accounts for the transformation from IT (the information age) to DT (the mass data age). In the IT era, the Internet was regarded as a tool, like "+ Internet". For example, when a piece of technology like the mobile phone accessed the Internet, it was known as "mobile phone + Internet" technology; when a security system used the Internet to offer visual access to a home via mobile phone, it was called a "smart door" with "secure door + Internet" technology.

Apple Inc. is a typical example of the upgrade from Internet to "Internet+". In overthrowing the previous concept of "mobile phone + Internet", Apple launched a new "Internet + mobile phone", creating an ecology of "Internet+". Although many people consider the iPhone simply to be a new mobile phone model, regarding it as a hardware revolution, Apple actually unleashed a completely new logic for "Internet+". Such logic is more clearly understood by comparing an iPhone with the mobile phones produced by Nokia or Motorola in the same year.

Nokia and Motorola mobile phones are "mobile phones + Internet", while Apple produces "Internet + mobile phone" technology. The sequence change indicates a brand new situation in which, via the Internet, mobile phones create a life that cannot be achieved by hardware alone.

In this sense, "DT" actually refers specifically to the way in which the mobile Internet facilitates limitless connectivity between people, allowing individuals to assume leading business roles, substituting traditional media with individual media, traditional channels with individual channels, traditional organizations with invidiual organizations and brands with individual brands. Individuals thus become the center of everything, creating a brand new world.

- Readers become part of the shared WeMedia, and change patterns of communication.
- Consumers become channels of industry and change patterns of business.
- Individuals become self-organizations and change patterns of management.
- "Friend Circles" become individual brands and change the pattern of consumer lifestyles.

Eight Breakthroughs: What is different about the Business Ecosystem of DT?

Breakthrough One: In the past, the leaders of business activities were enterprises, while today the protagonists are individuals within the DT ecosystem.

While enterprises were previously at the forefront of business systems, today, individuals have taken the place of enterprises via the mobile Internet. For example, WeMedia allows the individual to take the lead in communication, and individual channels (such as micro-businesses) empower individuals to guide industrial channels. Individual branding allows an individual to stand as the face of their own "product" or "market", and even business organizations have been reoriented around self-organized individuals.

Breakthrough Two: Before, there were commercial business products; now, there are commercial operators of the DT ecology in operational tribes.

In the past, traditional business models were run around a product, and inventory was a huge problem, necessitating the creation and stockpiling of products based on demand. In the traditional business model, companies were required to either imagine the needs of others, or spend heavily on forcible promotional advertising, making it a challenge to keep the focus on customers.

In the mobile Internet DT era, business operations are carried out around tribes. What is a tribe? Tribes refer to groups of people with common interests, hobbies and values. With the tribe as the center, customer needs and lifestyles are accounted for in the creation of products, giving rise to C2B (customer to business) reverse custom products and destroying the need for inventory – a truly customer-centric achievement.

Breakthrough Three: In the past, business followed the logic of self-benefit; nowadays DT business ecology follows the altruistic logic of benefiting others. The logic of DT is about correlation, while the traditional business logic is about causality. Correlation is about one's ecological ideology, while causality stands for egotistical linear thought. Put well by Jack Ma, IT is self-strengthening, while DT strengthens others; the IT era allowed others to serve individuals, while DT puts business in the hands of the people.

But how exactly does "DT" emphasize the strengthening of others and a desire to help others succeed? Because in the DT era we all live in the same ecology, and if we help others to be strong, the whole system will be strong.

Breakthrough Four: In the past, the pursuit of business was about popularity; now, DT business ecology involves the pursuit of niche personalities.

In the past, popularization and standardization were the chief goals of a business on the road to excellence. Every enterprise made efforts to pursue masses of users, tending towards standardization and large-scale expansion. Especially in the PC (personal computer) era, all e-businesses were striving to gain tens of millions of users, developing business into a game of burning money.

Today the business strategy of mobile e-commerce is just the opposite. Such businesses do not pursue mass-quantity users but high-quality users. Mobile e-commerce operators do not "burn money", but what they do burn is time. Mobile social media platforms such as Facebook and WeChat are primarily concerned with emotion and identity. With customer identities at hand, business activities find new ways in, including the ability to reverse customize a product according to individual consumer needs. This refers to the C2B model mentioned above.

Breakthrough Five: In the past, consumers were controlled commercially through the media; today, the DT commercial ecology uses the media to embrace users.

In the days of B2C commerce, vertical forms of communication prevailed, meaning that enterprises were at the top, with consumers at the bottom under the control of the media. Enterprises bought advertising time in which they organized and planned product information with which to indoctrinate consumers. With such a mode of communication, the largest companies were able to gain much more power than small counterparts.

The DT business ecology today largely involves horizontal C2C (Customer to Customer) communication, as users no longer trust enterprises, but trust other users. This is part of what has been called the WeMedia era. WeMedia gives a voice to everyone through a mobile phone and other wearable equipment, allowing every consumer to speak, and ending the era of corporate control over information and communication.

Breakthrough Six: In the past, businesses saw the channel as king; the DT business ecology regards individual channels (WeBusiness) as king.

In the product era, inventory was within the producing business; in the market era, inventory was in channels; and in the mobile Internet era, inventory lies in a user's home. Wherever inventory lies, business competition finds its core; all competition is centered around consumer demands, and a channel is simply a bridge between product and consumer. When inventory is within an enterprise, the product is king; when inventory is in a channel, that channel is king; when inventory is inside a user's home, the user stands as both king and channel. This is the emergence of micro-business or WeBusiness.

The appearance of WeChannels indicates an economic sharing of talent, where consumers and enterprises take part-time roles in business. All parties involved are entitled to gain profits from sales and services. Furthermore, such consumer talent may lead to enterprise partnerships, allowing individuals to participate in production, design and profit in a market of "crowd-sourced innovation". Customers can become the enterprise's partners and gain profits from the market of "crowd-sourced innovation".

Breakthrough Seven: In the past, business was operated by organizations; now, DT business ecologies are run in a self-organizing manner (WeOrganization)

Nature and the market system are typical examples of self-organizing models, emphasizing self-healing mechanisms without the need for excessive external intervention. In so-called "WeOrganizations", the mobile Internet revives this natural ecological model, using self-organizational models rather than formal organization as in traditional enterprises. This, in recent years, has led to the emergence of new economic forms such as "public investment", "crowdfunding" and "crowd-sourced innovation". Furthermore, such organization has also led to the replacement of traditional channels with micro-businesses as the commercial protagonist. In this sense, "Internet+" stands to spark a "management revolution", with larger-scale enterprises having the most difficulty in adaptation.

Breakthrough Eight: In the business ecology of the past, brands belonged to enterprises; now, the DT business ecology puts brands in the hands of the user, engendering the "We Brand".

In the past, brands belonged to enterprises, as enterprises spread information through the media, rendering the consumer passive. In the DT era, brands belong to users, which I call the time of the "We Brand". In the era of mobile Internet, users produce trust in a product. As the center of business activity has been transferred from objects to people, and property rights to human rights, people have replaced enterprises as the protagonists of economic activity, replacing companies as the leader of marketing activities. Now, everyone can be a brand.

CHAPTER 2

REDEFINING MOBILE E-COMMERCE FROM A HUMAN PERSPECTIVE

Today, the mobile Internet is first concerned with transforming "the state of existence" and then the business itself. Take the Chinese market for example, in which many products that do not seem suitable for e-commerce models, such as clothing and furniture, have become the largest categories of the Chinese e-commerce sector. In 2015, online shopping transactions amounted to a total of nearly 4 trillion RMB in China, of which online clothing sales accounted for 20%, the highest ranking online market, as compared with 2008, in which clothing accounted for merely 1.8% of the online market.

In just four years, e-commerce has overthrown the entire apparel retail industry. Why? Clearly this is not simply explained by network technology, but reflects the irrational structure of the traditional Chinese markets that involve an over-reliance on real estate, with extreme differences between urban and rural areas, excessive manufacturing and a serious shortage of services.

This shows that the power of e-commerce, as based on the Internet, is not limited to technical adaptations, but the implication of a completely different business logic to that of the traditional enterprise. In other words, e-commerce has subverted the "spatial logic" that traditional business has relied on for centuries.

What is said "spatial logic" of the traditional business? Take clothing as an example. In the current Chinese business structure, if the retail price of a garment is less than 6-8 times the ex-factory price (seller's selling cost), it will incur loss. In comparison, the money one may spend on one piece of clothing at a shopping mall could perhaps pay for multiple pieces of clothing online.

This demonstrates the basic logic of current e-commerce development; successful categories for e-commerce sales, such as garments, cosmetics, furniture, and building materials, all share one characteristic: huge differences between their ex-works prices and retail prices, which ultimately drives the rapid development of these categories.

Now we must ask, how did this huge difference come about? The answer refers to the "spatial logic" of traditional commerce.

Traditional commerce resulting from the Industrial Revolution was dependent on three basic spatial elements: rent, channels and advertizing. We want to ask how this huge balance is formed. This is what I call the "Spatial Logic" of the traditional business. The traditional business created by the industrial revolution relies on three basic spatial elements: locality, marketing and access channel, which may be called the "three new big mountains". In traditional business ecology, any enterprise that hopes to access the market and develop must first surmount these "three new big mountains".

The first mountain is about locality and rent. The great development of contemporary business is closely related to urbanization, and in order to sell products a business must occupy urban centers, i.e. shopping malls. How do shopping malls exist? With a reliance on rent. Where does this rent come from? The merchants. If a business merchant cannot pay rent, one effectively loses a "passport" to access the market.

The second mountain regards marketing. Competition lies within the market, and the communication of advertisements is necessary in gaining consumer interest in one's products. Marketing communication is also very expensive, and in viewing the annual advertizing revenue of TV marketing enterprises, one will understand what marketing means to a business.

The third mountain is related to channels. In order to make a business strong and powerful, one must exert the utmost strength to occupy more areas, or channels, while offering more sales and services, all of which require professional people for operation. In China, so-called "Channel Kings" refer to businesses like Wal-Mart, Suning, Gome and Wanda, which have already become the dominant forces of the market.

When we say that the ratio between the ex-factory price and the retail price of a garment is 6-8, the cost of these "three big mountains" of rent, advertizement and channel account for a major part of the apparel value chain.

People often neglect this key point, which has resulted in a dilemma for Chinese traditional channel giants when transitioning to e-commerce. On the one hand, traditional channels have seen the impact of e-commerce and hope to break into the O2O (Online to Offline) market, and on the other hand, when this so-called O2O environment is based in vested interests and a transformation to e-commerce that attempts to maintain traditional patterns of interest, it is ultimately futile.

The "Ethical Finance" of Mobile Providers

Ethics are concerned with good and evil, right and wrong. The Internet itself is people-focused rather than product-focused; it is attentive to hobbies and values rather than resources. In such a new ecological environment, any interest must have a level of "morality":

if it damages personal interests, it is unfair to private morality; if it harms everyone's interests, it is fraudulent to public morality.

Thus we may see the other side of competition in e-commerce: on the surface is a dispute of interests, behind which is a battle of honesty and morality. All e-commerce businesses in the pursuit of success are invariably focused on integrity and morality, as we can see in Amazon and T-mall: desperately conjuring customer service that will be exchanged for praise.

Of course, some may say that certain businesses pay and hire an "online water army" to purchase such praise. Is this fraud? Certainly, and this "water army" does exist, but how might the Internet combat such fraud? This is where the era of social media platforms such as Facebook and WeChat quietly comes in.

How does a business participate in e-commerce through social media platforms such as Facebook, Line or WeChat? Although there are no explicit answers to this question as of now, it seems that it is only a matter of time before C2C mobile e-commerce based on the social platforms take the place of B2C modes like Amazon and T-mall, ultimately becoming the most mainstream form of e-commerce.

At present, the biggest difference between social media platform C2C and market B2C e-commerce is the replacement of merchants with individuals, as in C2C individuals take the leading role in business activities. Once commerce is lead by people rather than enterprises, moral power will take a key position. Here's one simple example: during earthquake disaster rescue processes, human power has gradually become more important. This is due to innovations in communication, in which social platforms on mobile phones are a major communication tool, and there is a resuscitation of social morals in "tribe ethics" on social media platforms: public places that naturally aggregate human "interests, hobbies and/or values".

As such, mobile commerce is inseparable from ethics. On mobile social platforms, any individual moral behavior is spread into each node of the network, becoming a public moral event; either in the form of "lightning deals" (a sales mode by which online merchants launch certain commodities at super low prices and all buyers simultaneously snap them up online); or in the circulation within niche tribes through "instant connections" (connecting all parties and spreading information in a very short time).

The biggest advantage of social platforms is the ability to record everyone's behavior, recorded by oneself as with the formation of WeChat or Line friend circles, or by others in browsing on Facebook or Twitter. In a word, when you have done a good thing or helped others, there will always be a record online.

In saying that, acts of both good and evil will be recorded. The record of evil actions will serve as the "Negative Brand" of the wrongdoer, and lead to Negative Equity in the future—"what goes around, comes around". So, the reason that merchants care about bad reviews on Amazon or T-mall is the negative asset created by a bad review. While a consumer may plan to purchase something, a bad review will pose an immediate obstacle.

In the same way, the records of good deeds are sure to become positive branding in the promise of future capital — "though my brother is not in the rivers and lakes, rivers and lakes tell the story of my brother". This is why "friend circles" on social media platforms are so crucial, because every person you contact through this circle of friends has a say in whether or not you are trustworthy.

In any case, any moral act by an individual or company will ultimately become "public ethics" or a "public ethic precedent", and positively impact the assets of the individual or company via communication. Likewise, any immoral behaviour will be noted as "immoral conduct" and result in indelible nightmares for individuals and/or companies involved.

In establishing this correlation, individuals and/or companies are more highly motivated to manage "ethics" and moral powers, and this is the meaning of "Ethical Finance".

The phrase "Ethical Finance" signifies a new ethical system that has been built in the mobile e-commerce era, reliant on a characteristic of "correct human behaviour", in which moral conduct is upgraded into assets with high ROI (return on investment) as a result of pervasive social communication.

In this world, no person is absolutely good or evil. Good

systems have the capacity to turn evil, and vice versa. The moral system behind mobile e-commerce may be capable of turning evil into good, and in this sense mobile e-commerce may be called an "economy for good".

Changing Times: E-commerce as the Fourth Revolution of Retail.

I grew up in the Chinese countryside, and in my memories of my childhood there was a weekly festival called "Gan Chang" in the local dialect, meaning "go to the market", referring to peasants who took homemade goods to the rural marketplace for trade.

When such market trade develops to a certain extent, new business forms appear in department stores. From a spatial viewpoint, a market is structured horizontally, with goods displayed over a space of the merchant's choosing, with the entire marketplace thus covering a huge amount of space. In a department store, on the other hand, space is developed vertically, and spatial shortages are solved by multi-level structuring, an intensive use of space.

The appearance of department stores was the first revolution of retail, with the trading market shifting from horizontal to vertical development, and the entrance into an era of intensive spatial management, which is to say that space became the scarcest resource of business. The second revolution in retail was the "Wal-

Mart Model", in which not only was space made even greater and commodity categories were completed, but, most importantly, a system of chain management was adopted alongside the formation of a powerful logistic supply chain.

The Commercial Complex was the third retail revolution. The difference between a "commercial complex" and the "Wal-Mart model" involved the inclusion of a cinema, ice rink, catering and even KTV within city complexes. A city complex turns a purely commercial system into a place with vital life.

The momentum that has propelled these three revolutions, from trade markets to department stores, department stores to supermarkets, then supermarkets to complex hypermarkets is called urbanization. As the scale of urban populations grows on a daily basis, business locations in centers are like pieces of gold, and rents are rising accordingly. As such, if merchants wish to gain consumer favor, they must compete for counters and shelves, all the while rent is increased by competition.

Another result of this business evolution is the creation of the so-called "brand". In the period of trade markets, there were no commodity brands, only brands based on acquaintance. Brands appeared in the period of the department store, and when it came to the models of Wal-Mart and larger complexes, brands became merchant marks, without which goods were not put on shelves.

Why have brands become more and more important in an era of industrialization? Not only because of commodity oversupply, but, more importantly, because sales space is limited. As public incomes increase, brands are not only a source of reputation, but a label of social status and prestige. Consequently, only well-known, large-scale brands are able to enter shopping malls in prime city center locations. High rent means that brands have gradually been gathered into the hands of only a few large enterprises. While brands, a result of market competition, are one of the greatest creations of the market, the "brand plus rent model" means that small enterprises are almost completely excluded from prime marketplaces.

To some, it appears that the biggest advantage of core companies such as Coca-Cola or McDonald's is the scale of their supply chains. However, this is just a superficial phenomenon. As the management costs of such big companies are extremely high, their biggest advantage is actually not in scale but in the monopoly of space, raw materials, key accessories and sales channels. In monopolizing supply chains and channels, small companies strive to provide supporting services for these huge enterprises, with distributors competing to become their agents and shopping malls prioritizing their access.

In this way, the environment makes it more and more difficult for small companies to survive. Throughout the 20th century, the most crucial evolutionary logic involved pushing the value of space to a maximum, with rent in shopping malls increasing continuously, and housing prices in central locations also rising perpetually. As most companies are located in high-class office buildings in city centers, citizens strive to live in the city center for more convenient access to enterprises and shopping malls. Such desire for convenience requires greater expenses, which is the essence of rising housing prices.

As a result, no matter how good a single product may be, if it is unable to enter a supermarket, commercial complex or exclusive shop, or even if it enters these areas but has no money for advertizement and promotion, it will surely be met with loss.

E-commerce is the current, fourth revolution of retail, and is focused on online shopping. For several hundred years, business competition has been carried out around central city "space", and online shopping has broken this spatial limitation for the first time. Without rent, entry fees or even the necessity of cash flow, the presale mode of payment before delivery has become dominant in e-commerce.

Suppose the model of "rent and shop" that business has relied on was broken down. What changes would occur? I believe that this essential problem has not been carefully considered until now, and this is why most past efforts of O2O (Online to Offline) have failed.

Chapter 3

RADICAL REFORM: HOW TO IDENTIFY TRUE OR FALSE O2O

When e-commerce challenges the rent strategy of traditional retail, clients one by one move to online shopping, and offline businesses are hard to sustain. At this time, the traditional business must resort to a coping strategy of O2O.

The logic of O2O is very simple: users move to online shopping, but they lack experience. O2O allows consumers to experience products firsthand and then purchase them online, engendering a cooperation between online and offline sales. Does this model not greatly increase the accuracy of clients in purchasing satisfactory products?

Upgraded O2O is known as scene-purchasing. When driving down a road, networks can recommend something that may interest you along the way, giving rise to a scene-demand. For example, when your car fuel is running out, technology can automatically recommend the location of nearby gas stations; when you're hungry, information about nearby restaurants appears. Google Glass is certainly the best platform for such scene-consumption.

In general, the discussion regarding O2O focuses on one core element, "purchase", in which no matter whether the purchase is based on experience or scene, the O2O environment allows users an easy payment method. Until now, most O2O based purchases have failed, and even O2O based on maps have made little breakthrough in the business environment.

Why is this? I believe that the difficulty lies in regarding O2O as a tool to keep hold of retail channels or "direct flow", without considering the essence of the Internet and the basic ecology of consumers' lives. In early 1996, Nicholas Negroponte, a professor at Massachusetts Institute of Technology, wrote *Being Digital*, which depicts a virtual and digital activity space in which future human beings will live "made up of bits". Since the birth of the human race, we have lived in a realistic physical space, but as mankind is beginning to establish virtual and digital spaces, information is taking the place of "bits" – atoms – as the new, essential DNA of human society.

In experiencing the innovation of the mobile Internet, we must renew our understanding of what is means to be "made up of bits". It is no longer an innovation of technology, but, just as Negroponte writes, "the reason why the Internet made of bits can absorb people is not only because it is a global, public network, but also because it has naturally evolved without the scheming of designers. There are no longer people issuing orders, but all its parts are progressing each day, which is amazing." Being "made up of bits" has created a brand new world. When using and studying social media platforms such as Facebook and WeChat, I feel that the world of networks may be the real world, and the realistic world only a virtual world that allows bodies to live. In the bit world of the Internet, people are enabled to express themselves honestly, each individual's "one face", according to Facebook.

In fact, with careful consideration this appears entirely logical. The atomic world is actually the entity world in which we live, a world which focuses on "material" things. We know that the basic meaning of a physical world is dependent on spatial limitations, and the "materialism" of the world is "pragmatism".

"Bits" of the mobile Internet, which I know as the real world, are emblematic of its transcendence of the limitations of space and materiality, granting freedom to the individual. To be clear on this point makes it easy to understand O2O in the mobile Internet area. O2O in the PC era still involved "atomic bits" (at the beginning and end of the line), and the focus was on how to make a computer better serve human beings at a higher efficiency, the core of customer-centric logic for profit gain.

On the other hand, O2O in the era of the Internet is a matter of "bits of atoms" (at the beginning and end of the line), where the key is to improve how the material world revolves around the needs of mankind. The mobile Internet is a way of life, with a business strategy that takes people as the central focus, rather than customers. At its core is the achievement of happiness for different tribes of people.

The Essence of O2O: Integration of Life and Business

According to market research by a firm called eMarketer, it is predicted that by 2018, the number of smartphone users in China will reach 700 million, accounting for nearly 1/3 of the total number of smart phone users worldwide. Mobile phones allow us to enter a life network, and humans have never been as they are today, with lifestyles and social relations moved to the Internet. Smartphones pioneered exactly this sense from which a brand new human lifestyle occurs. A large number of commercial facilities and life services will be reconstructed due to this change in lifestyle, and this is the backdrop for the performance of O2O.

In a qualitative leap, we as humans are fortunate enough to live "made of bits", moving from an atomic existence to a bit existence.

As a result, the Internet no longer simply proposes purchases and business activities, but offers an entire new way of life. This way of life has only just begun, but with the development of artificial intelligence, large numbers of purely online life practices are constantly being created.

As human life has become "made of bits", its most prominent element has proven to be the "speed of light" with which information flows uninterrupted, enabling information to greatly benefit consumers once it is decentralized. As the connection of personal media has become the mainstream mode of information dissemination, everyone is not only a disseminator of information, but also a consumer, breaking previous barriers of information asymmetry. With these barriers breaking down, management models that rely on asymmetric information, such as pyramid schemes, channel agency models and advertising promotional models, are all faced with enormous challenges.

Openness and transparency of information is creating a whole new dimension of human aggregation and space itself, and this is the spatial element of O2O. The value of space does not disappear, but it no longer revolves around sales channels like commercial complexes. Experiential consumption, such as cinemas, restaurants and entertainment venues are no longer simply locations of spillway in the flow of consumption, but are areas where fans gather and communicate. Business is no longer centralized in the commercial complex, but in the consumers themselves; business no longer aims to operate commodities, but to manage fans.

When the value of merchant management is greater than the value of doing business, the value of online communities is clear. For example, China's leading mobile operator, Xiaomi, had its biggest breakthrough in the creation of a "go-to-channel" for O2O business. Such a brand new ecology means that managing fans and assessing how people spend their time is key for new business models.

Here, human time becomes the most valuable asset, and the element of time has since become the core element of competition across the mobile Internet, from which we can imagine that the value of time must exceed that of space.

Once time has become the central element of business competition, the rules of the game in which firms compete are changed. First comes people, then business; first demand, then supply. Such a new ecology has the capacity to greatly reduce the cost of living for a company, not to mention the greater potential for resource sharing provided by cloud computing. For example, a Chinese start-up company is able to rent within the Aliyun cloud service system, create tens of millions of dollars of revenue, and only pay a cloud service fee of 75 RMB per month. In the past, to achieve the same kind of profit would require tens of millions of dollars in equipment costs.

The Chinese government is aware of this potential, too. As a result, stringent requirements have been lifted regarding registered capital in business administration. Even the requirements for acceptable business premises have been broadened. Anyone with a proposition of unique value can now create and serve a niche tribe of consumers by aggregating such tribes over the mobile Internet, ultimately allowing smaller companies to survive.

In this age of the Internet, the main body of business can be a single person alone, and even if this person only runs a part-time business, the wealth and value they create will not necessarily be small. With boundaries between companies and consumers disappearing, consumer engagement is changing the traditional concept of "company scale".

"Group Field Theory": The Closed-Loop of O2O

People have a notion of sociality; that is, they try to live in accordance with community values. While such values may be one's own choice, they may also be imposed by society. "Internet+" intends to express such a way of life, in which the Internet offers freedom to choose in a "tribal life".

O2O's "group theory" is as follows: based on a group life "made of bits", people are grouped together at similar frequencies. Based on atomized fields of life, people at the same frequency have the same emotional response, and the field of O2O forms a closed loop. This is a closed-loop based on lifestyle, not a closed-loop of sales. When O2O is closed around life, sales become a much more simple matter.

Such a rise of O2O to the level of life is a result of the emergence of a new ecology over the mobile Internet, allowing people to gather in space in a totally new way. Through the mobile Internet, virtual spatial aggregation and lifestyle changes have been made, with humans as the first beings in history to achieve borderless contact.

Indeed, mankind has never before existed in the same virtual space as we do today, in which we have realized the convergence of interests, hobbies and values. Here, the result of such aggregation is what we call a "group". With regards to any mobile product, it can be said that if there is no "group", it is not e-commerce.

Why do people like to give themselves nicknames on the Internet? I believe that this is not entirely out of a need for anonymity. Indeed, from a sociological point of view, the name is a symbol of a person's characteristics, and therefore as an Internet nickname is completely self-selected, it presents a psychological "projection". One looks to the kind of person they are, or how one expects others to see them, then expresses a yearning which is then reflected in a self-designated web name.

So, behind any screen name, there is a "self-pursuit" of certain interests, hobbies or values. We all know that things come together;

people gather in groups or networks, in which this "self-pursuit" is a major turning point. With the popularization of smartphones, people are enabled to communicate online at any time, and the era of the "group" has arrived.

This is a brand new human movement, but it is a migration that did not occur in geographical space, but over a virtual social network. The movement is not of people in pursuit of more suitable natural environments, but in pursuit of ways to live among people who share similar interests, hobbies and values.

Man is a highly developed social animal, and in determining the people in his life, looks for his own kind as a prerequisite for happiness. People are also a species with diverse needs, meaning that they play different roles in different environments in the overall pursuit of their dreams. Superimposing these two conditions manifests the value of the "group". It is a case of looking for a "group" based on similarity, while necessitating a wide variety of such "groups" due to a need for diversity.

However, people are, after all, a harmonious amalgam of body and spirit. When people form tribes in virtual groups, and create a culture around this "spirit", they naturally have a need to meet, and there is a motivation to consolidate communal happiness, which creates the "field". If the group is "made of bits", in a digitized state of existence, then the "field" is a group of atoms.

In Chinese, "field" means either a place where many people gather and move, or it refers to the distribution of an object in space.

The chief attribute of a field is that it occupies a space. An electric field, for example, is an aggregation of electrons distributed across a certain space. A magnetic field is a special form produced by an accumulation of atoms in space. The "business field", or "market", is a gathering of people and things involving spatial transactions.

A group is the premise of a field. This is not a field where people casually converge, but a specific locale for the convergence of online communities, a kind of active venue for a group of people with strong relationships, a "camp" or "home".

Such is the relationship between the group and the field, the basis for the O2O model, a relationship that clearly shows the group as a prerequisite for a field, where being online is a valuable premise for offline activity.

Relationships that people form online and offline are different, the biggest difference being that online relationships are more pure. On the Internet, two strangers meet, and without much understanding of one another's background, faces or voices, they are able to communicate with each other with far less concern for such scruples.

This kind of Internet communication causes distress to certain "big shots", as the halos of their offline reputations are missing. A person who is sensational in the real world may not be so on the Internet.

Think of this basic sociological theory: "labelling theory". Howard Becker, who proposed this labelling theory, points out that groups with the power of discourse will define those without such a power, and may even impose some negative features of identity on the latter.

The biggest issue with labelling theory is its proposal of "social compaction", also known as "identity inheritance". When lower or middle class individuals accept the labels imposed by the social mainstream, controlled by those with more social power, they review their own behavior by such standards, and the mentality and actions of the lower classes are "compacted".

Such is the power of a "field". When a "field" determines a group, society is compacted. When "friends" of the same field meet online, they will first review one another by known social labels, which then determines the course of any following offline communication. When a group determines a field, however, society will flow more freely, as it is based on pure online relationships in which people do not review one another by social labels, but form relationships according to hobbies and values.

Fields based on groups have engendered a new social labelling system. What will happen when people operate on the same frequency and gather together? They will create new leading styles of living, behavioral modes, value concept systems and punishment systems.

In short, the offline field encourages the change of a person, while the online group selects people as they are. Selection is greater than change, and this is a fundamental pattern of social life that exists as a reason for the mainstream implementation of tribal we-channels and mobile e-commerce. Life is short; it is not important for a person to change themselves in a limited timeline, but to select like-minded companions with whom to walk through life together.

Such an analysis allows us to realize that traditional frameworks of analysis do not work in today's world, as users are not able to aggregate across the Internet, forming "tribes" or "groups" amidst the renewed business ecology of the DT era. In this time, any business analysis must start from online life patterns, and then realize offline modes. Life is bigger than business, and to create life is to create business.

CHAPTER 4

LIFE IS GREATER THAN BUSINESS: THE INNOVATIVE LOGIC OF TRIBES

People refer to Facebook, Twitter, Weibo and WeChat as "social media" due to the living, rather than technical, nature of such systems. When it came to electronic platforms in the PC area, people talked about how to be good sellers on Amazon, Lynx and Taobao, or how to promote on Google. In the DT era, however, social e-commerce is based on a life perspective. It considers how to enhance interpersonal relationships, and how to improve the efficiency and identification of interpersonal communication.

I believe this is an important transition, which I would like to emphasize. The biggest breakthrough for mobile commerce is its basis on life itself as both the starting point and end result. Mobile operators run lifestyles rather than just business.

Today's success stories of Internet business are gradually shifting towards smaller businesses and individuals with dreams. The Internet, especially the mobile form, has broken the boundaries between life and business by turning those who love life into business moguls. The future generation of business tycoons will no longer be the most proficient businesspeople, but those who love life.

Creativity does not come entirely from individuals, but has to do with the environment in which a person lives. The great thing about the mobile Internet is the creation of a virtual living environment (this is the real O2O, which I will discuss further later), and any given environment will produce certain concepts and actions.

Human beings, as social animals, determine their happiness based on their environments and the people around them. If one lived alone on a desert island, even with riches and power, where would happiness arise? The greatness of the mobile Internet lies in its cultivation of a virtual living space, and it may already be said that we live in such social networks.

At the very least, the Internet helps us maintain social relationships. Today, the best way to connect with friends and family members is through social media networks, which most people are a part of. This is the most important aspect of this era of mobile commerce, in which people have realized online social platforms (environments) that transcend space and time.

Why is the value of communication so important? Gustave Le Bon puts it aptly, in "The Crowd: A Study of the Popular Mind", stating, "when it comes to emotion, the gaps between people disappear."

The elimination of gaps in status through emotion is the core of the small-scale logic of the Internet age: rather than emphasizing the social gaps between people, it emphasizes emotions shared by people. Alongside this sentiment is the contrary logic of large-scale interest: emphasizing wealth, status and identity rather than interpersonal feelings.

The next question is what the future may look like for the mobile e-commerce providers that emphasize emotion. At this point, I must not fail to mention the dilemma facing the commercialization of social platforms: the natural exclusion of social platforms from commerce. On such platforms, it only takes one advertizement or promotion for some to be disgusted, and if WeChat friend circles are full of advertizing information, the attractiveness of such circles will decline.

Indeed, social platforms such as Facebook and WeChat have triggered impacts on every industry. However, these platforms have yet to make substantial breakthroughs in the development of e-commerce, and numerous companies and individuals looking to do business through WeChat have found this platform ill-suited for business activities.

The commercial dilemma facing social platforms demonstrates that traditional business models cannot be precisely transported to mobile platforms. Mobile social media platforms are emotion-based communication tools, that is, human platforms, rather than business platforms based purely on monetary interest. Although the foundation has changed, the way in which people do business has not, and a predicament naturally arises.

At the depths of a crisis lies opportunity. Put another way, the jump from B2C logic to C2C or C2B logics may seem to promise a "new continent": people expanding contacts based on social platforms, the realization of a long-held traditional desire for "customer traffic", with people converging into groups with interests, hobbies and values. Is this not the "customer traffic" that marketers have always dreamed of?

Over the years, marketing has pursued two propositions, the first being how to induce customer traffic, the second being how to accurately analyze customer needs and provide a clear customer base, thereby providing consumers with products they need. Today, customers arrive as individuals and organize themselves into groups, yet merchants are unsure how to respond.

This issue involves an important transferral of power, as in the past, business rules were enterprise-led, while now the individual prevails. Enterprises no longer have the power to interfere in customer groups, which are under the control of customers themselves. Such a difference (indeed, the most essential difference) has posed an insurmountable obstacle for most traditional businesses, as it is not just a challenge to play the game, but to understand and abide by the rules of the game.

With customers in control, the mobile Internet creates a "niche logic", and the spring of "Long Tail products" arises alongside traditional logics of mass. Niche groups are gathering in the convergence of specific interests or values that are naturally "special", previously unable to enter a production market based purely on mass consumption.

Such is an example of user-oriented C2B logic, which is also behind the concepts of "crowdfunding" or "crowd creation". People come together on the basis of hobbies and interests, and generate demands for particular, custom products as a result of such interests. Due to the demand for customization, extreme innovation will occur.

Innovation is a Living Thing, Niche is Mass

More than a decade ago, I was the strategy manager at Motorola, and at that time my department at Motorola's Asia-Pacific branch wrote a report predicting that in the future, SMS business would become a larger means of business in China. Its revenue, we suggested, may even exceed that of voice calls.

At that time, the company executives thought the report was strange. How was this possible? United States mobile phone production was high in those days, with very few people using mobile messaging, strongly favoring voice messages instead.

However, a few years later, in China, SMS has proven the most important profit point for mobile phone companies. At ten cents per message, Chinese New Year alone could accrue billions of dollars. For more than ten years, the price of voice messages has gotten lower and lower, but the price of text messages has yet to reduce substantially. Profits gained by text messages by far surpass those of voice messages.

This is a story of innovation: why is such innovation so difficult to accept? United States Professor Geoffrey Moore has put forward a theory of "the chasm" in regards to the innovative products of high-tech enterprises. At its core, the theory proposes that there is a huge gap between "small-scale interests" and "the mainstream", a glitch in the system that makes it a challenge for technological innovations to become popular products, and the most crucial element of any technology company's business strategy is discovering how to cross this chasm.

Innovation in a mobile Internet environment is different namely due to the entrance into an era of "tribes". In such an era, innovation is like the growth of a child; it is no longer a profession, but a continuation of life itself. For example, in today's tribe of programmers, extremely advanced programs are a part of life from which they derive happiness and experience, gain dignity and accomplishment, rather than simply an exhibition of professional skill.

Surely, some people may suggest that this niche programmer phenomenon existed previously. So why has this phenomenon only now been publicised, changing the environment for innovation? This is because the mobile Internet has created "instantaneous" transmission. In the past, hundreds, thousands or perhaps even millions of programmers were scattered around the world, basically isolated from one another.

However, "instant connection" as enabled by mobile phones now empowers any individual programmer's behaviour to spread across the world in no time, creating an environment of "seamless" communication. Programmers around the world can communicate in real-time via mobile phone, in a mode of communication even simpler and more efficient than face-to-face contact.

Think of the World Cup: is it not because of live television that fans have been allowed to join together across the world? Now, with a mobile phone in one's hand, the equivalent of a handheld TV, live events can be broadcasted around the world. How many tribes of people with different interests and hobbies may this create?

Such is the principle of niche markets, in other words, innumerable "niches" created through the Internet as it operates across mobile phones and other wearable devices. When minorities of people converge across the world via the Internet, the so-called "mass" market disappears. Within each niche tribe, the niche may appear to be not just the general public, but the whole world.

This is completely new ground for innovation and growth, as the individuality and unconventionality of each minority tribe becomes the standard of life within that tribe; or, to put it more simply, things that appear remarkable in the frame of mass society become normal and mainstream within the frame of the niche.

On the contrary, those who are tribe "enthusiasts", a niche dedicated to the love of life, constitute the headquarters of innovation. At its foundation, the most important rule in the game of mobile e-commerce is that it is a "game of life", rather than a "game of profit". Members of tribes are productive and gain happiness simply from participation, and such results cannot be paid for or produced by a company, so self-organized tribal micro-commerce (WeCommerce) businesses are unmatched by traditional companies.

Of course, the other cost of tribal WeCommerce is very high, that is interest, or the cost of hobbies and values. Such costs require time, truth and long-term interactivity with people. So, if not an enthusiast of tribal life, one is basically unable to sustain WeCommerce business, and traditional big businesses find themselves in a strange new world.

In this world, the rules of the game are no longer based on money and interest, but emotion and identity; they no longer require organized management and control, but self-organized aggregation and integration. In short, the mobile Internet has revived the soil for innovation, and in the case of tribal WeCommerce, innovation is no longer a professional achievement, but an active interest of tribal life.

When we think of innovation as a way of doing business, innovation is no longer dominated by companies, but by the lives of groups of innovators. Here, innovation has tilled the soil of its existence and growth. Life is innovation, and innovation is the growth of life.

CHAPTER 5

TIME IS GREATER THAN SPACE: THE TIME ECONOMY HAS ARRIVED

During Spring Festival in 2014, I returned to Guizhou, my home province in the Southwest of China, and felt very happy to sit beside my 80-year-old mother. Perhaps this feeling was a continuation of the thousand-year-old feelings of Chinese people, in which a mother is home, and the children are just "migratory birds".

When I left Beijing, I found that on weekdays, even the most prosperous city was basically empty. This year, WeChat developed a popular feature: "red envelopes", based on the envelopes Chinese people offer one another each year during Spring Festival. These red envelopes offer good fortune and symbolize the festivities. In the spring of 2014, WeChat moved this tradition to the mobile phone.

The underlying premise of WeChat's "red envelopes" was simple, that is, to connect a person's bank card with the WeChat payment system, so as to convert bank payments to a mobile support system. Amidst China's powerful banking system, which has monopolized the economic center of China for many years, in a moment WeChat opened a gap!

And what did WeChat do in the end? It did nothing – just gave people the chance to send a red envelope, a traditional practice during a traditional Chinese festival. Strangely enough, WeChat did not pay a penny, as money went straight from the accounts of handset users.

But did WeChat and its program operators really not do anything? Perhaps this is not entirely true. WeChat revived the traditional sense of interpersonal relationships. Chinese people today do not live amongst companies or families, but in communities on WeChat. If what WeChat resurrected is the interaction between people, all the while transcending time and space, then, as a core point of interpersonal contact during China's Spring Festival, perhaps it has become a grand WeChat Festival.

Yes, when these WeChannel red envelopes were launched, major mobile phone companies were in despair, as on New Year WeChat messaging replaced SMS, capturing a huge potential profit pool. Faced with trembling bankers and crying mobile company CEOs, I would now like to discuss how a small mobile application like WeChat can have such a powerful influence.

Business Hours: a BUSINESSPERSON'S Sense of Happiness

Sociological studies have long shown that human well-being is closely related to "time". Thousands of years of evolution in human civilization can, in fact, be simplified into two elements: the value of space and the value of time. Space represents scarce resources, such as how the physical city embodies space. The formation of the city is a result of a market that requires an accumulation of people and things in space, and the price of malls as trading floors is getting higher and higher, which in turn is the reason for rising commercial real estate valuations, as well as prices within stores themselves.

By the same token, at the center of human life is the major activity of shopping. As a result, prices of housing near shopping centers is rising, and this is all from a perspective of space. When it comes to time, these situations are variable. For example, at Christmas, or Spring Festival in China, people are no longer concentrated on and in work, but on and in family. For example, every Chinese New Year, almost all prosperous cities are empty.

Where are people going? They are going "home".

Why go home? The answer is "happiness". Why is there no time to return home at other times, yet Spring Festival is filled with such happiness? The answer is that human happiness is closely related to certain "points in time", such as holidays or anniversaries.

Sociological studies have shown that human beings, over the evolutionary process, have invented a simple way to create happiness, and that is to give value to certain points in time. For example, a child's birthday, a wedding or an anniversary. In a community, common points of value recognized by people become collective or tribal festivals, such as Christmas in the West, or China's Spring Festival, Qing Ming, etc.

We all know that life is made up over time, not just in space. It is in this vein that "time is life". Time is continuous, and its continuity means that the value of time or life cannot be measured simply. As a result, humans have invented values in life, measuring time value in a weighted way. Such is the value of the festival, which represents neither money nor material wealth, but a special event at a specific time, a "day". Festivals are the permanent "memorial" of the value of a given day, because on this day, life is changed in value from that of ordinary, continuous time. It is a special event.

A child's birthday implies the reward of new life for children, parents, relatives and friends. Such meaning is the value of life itself, not relying on or even related to material wealth.

When the production of this kind of value exists on a group level, we can understand the origins of festivals like Spring Festival. Chinese New Year refers to the Lunar New Year's Day in the Chinese Lunar Calendar. The Chinese have endowed this festival with meanings of "family reunion" and ancestral worship. As a result, Spring Festival has become the most important moment for every family in China. Happiness in this moment can be enjoyed equally, regardless of who you are.

It is worth considering that Spring Festival may even be happier for the poor than the rich, more for the everyman than the elite. Such a conclusion is important, as it points at a hidden truth that business is a departure from life. For centuries, the industrial revolution, with spatial resources at the core of competition, has propelled a kind of departure from human nature, proposing what has been dubbed "possession or abandonment" (the cost of safeguarding wealth is high, causing people to give up the pursuit of meaning in life), "shackled by desire" (when people become slaves to desire).

All of this is rooted in the basic restraints of wealth created by the industrial revolution, that is, the fact that market transactions must happen in certain real spaces. As a result, the market has become the channel for competition, and competition for this channel entails nothing more than contests over mall shelves and through television and newspaper advertizing. Rising housing prices as well as television and newspaper advertizing costs are simply an inevitable conclusion, creating television advertizement superstars.

The Internet has changed all of this with online shopping department stores, as shopping centers have lost all purpose. Even if shopping centers do exist, they stand as places for experience and face-to-face service, not an essential place for trading. At any rate, we should not underestimate two forces: the first being science and technology, the other human nature. Today's mobile Internet is formed partially of technology (removing the need for physical market transaction space), and partially on human nature (the business of time).

So, the question now is: is this good news or bad news?

For countless entrepreneurs and small businesses, this is good news, while it is bad news for "famous brands" that have been standardized and popularized. The popularity of a niche product like WeChat red envelopes indicates that we are in an era of human nature, in which the nature of people tends towards individuality and minority values. Industrial trends towards standardization and popularization are declining.

Over the next ten years, we may indeed witness the decline of standardized mass brands such as McDonald's and KFC, with the mobile Internet focused not on "mass" but on more human "niches". The spring of small business and entrepreneurship has arrived – a pluralistic world no longer dominated by a handful of big brands.

Where There is Time, There is Value

The biggest difference in social e-commerce as opposed to traditional business is the social aspect; it is people-oriented, based primarily on the relationships between people, meaning that social e-commerce operators spend 99% of their time on people, and 1% of their time on sales, with every moment offering the potential for multiplied sales. But what exactly is this business model?

In fact, this question is posed incorrectly, and should be: as a unique individual, how are you willing to spend your time? Are you willing to spend time purchasing goods, or would you rather spend time on your interests, hobbies or values?

Yes, by placing life above business, social e-commerce providers are enabled to gain permits in the DT era, formed on a basis of "tribal" interest, hobbies and values. The value of any kind of lifestyle is determined by a specific group of people. For example, Spring Festival is integral to Chinese people, while for others around the world it may just be an ordinary day. This is known as "value relativity".

Value relativity is the source of finance. If the value of something is the same for everyone, then there is no opportunity for exchange, and without exchange there is no "premium". In creating diverse lifestyle channels, the mobile Internet heralds in a concrete financial age. All businesses created through the Internet are, in essence, aimed at creating "brand value" in their products.

Allow me to illustrate this point by first discussing a specific case.

In China, a shop exists that sells roses via the Internet. The price of roses is high, but the business remains successful. The message of the store is: "buy these for only one person in your lifetime", and when you buy a rose, you must provide the store with the recipient's ID number. From that point on, for as long as you return to the store to buy roses, you may only buy flowers for this one person, meaning you will not be able to give another person a rose from this store for the rest of your life.

This is an interesting case study. What is special about it is the idea of business based completely on "human values", as it cleverly uses the loyalty of love to maximize the uniqueness of the roses.

Of course, one could also say that this is simply a clever, differentiated marketing strategy. On the surface this may be true, but think about it: could such differentiation really be possible without the Internet? A model is established in the knowledge that people who buy flowers prefer to shop for them online than offline. Only with online shopping as a pervasive business model are "once in a lifetime" purchases made possible.

On the other hand, this store is less about business and more about flowers, and by taking a view on love, it is not so much a business, but more an "abduction or coercion of love", in which men are required to love only one woman over the course of their lives. Is this a business or a promotion of a concept of love?

In any case, this case confirms the previous argument that the most significant change brought about by the mobile Internet is the grasp of life before business, or even that existence on the mobile Internet is life itself. When one's hobbies, interests and values are the core elements of product "premiums", lifestyles also gain "financial value".

So-called "value relativity" proposes that value is relative, and the value in any item is determined by the number of people who come into contact with it. The more individuals who come into contact with it, and the wider the breadth of preferences of those people, the more easily the value of said item will appear. Here, the revolutionary significance of the mobile Internet emerges, as it brings us into a world of "instantaneous connection", in which all people and things are "united".

By all means, this indicates that we are not bound to an infinite number of other people, and with infinite numbers of people engaged in the Internet, the pursuit of uniqueness in mankind is certain to engender "financial value" for all things: what is useless to you may be meaningful to others; what was once useless may no longer be useless in the future.

As in the above case of the rose shop, the value of the product is fundamentally changed when considered under the guise of "once in a lifetime". Obviously this concept works here, as it has a clear attachment to "the love of one's life". However, this is not a concept that everyone agrees upon, or to put it differently, those who agree with the sentiment are the target customers of this rose shop.

With the value of roses as a starting point, this "one in a lifetime" sales business model is not about the evaluation of roses themselves, but an attitude of love, a way of judging the value of love. Selling roses is a business, but "once in a lifetime" is a life evaluation. When people purchase flowers, it is not only a lifestyle choice between lovers, but a promise and organization of the future.

Life doesn't happen in the past, but moves into the future. Why is it that the elderly have experienced more time, but tend to be more dissatisfied with life? Why do young people always look toward the future? This is the value of "freedom", which we pursue as an unknown, full of dreams. If the future was known, what would be the point of life?

When time, rather than space, is at the core of business competition, the business model of the mobile Internet DT era proves people-centered, rather than customer-focused, and customers are just a product of the past B2C era. In the social era of C2C, there are no customers, only people.

CHAPTER 6

TRIBAL WECHANNEL E-COMMERCE: E-COMMERCE OF THE PEOPLE

Science and technology not only lead the world with technological productivity, but also lead in the creation of new lifestyles. Take Facebook, Twitter, WeChat, Weibo, or various online games, for example, in which little technical innovation is occurring, yet revolutionary breakthroughs are taking place from the perspective of interpersonal socialization. At present, humans have begun to live online.

In traditional models of industrialization, the value of a product was artificially reduced to "price/function ratio", as people were gradually separated from one another and/or communication between people was limited. Merchants using such business models utilized "cost performance" to strictly limit the value of products to their functional value, or replaced the value of consumer interactivity with the social status of a "brand".

Facebook, Twitter, Weibo and WeChat are platforms that no longer regard product value as the core of e-commerce, as e-commerce sees value in people, with social media companies at the mainstream of mobile Internet use, and with people replacing the "product" as the protagonist of business communities. Now, the problem is that business has undergone such fundamental change, and with people still accustomed to using "price" or "brand" to measure product value, mobile providers have yet to achieve a revolutionary breakthrough.

I have put forward the term "tribal WeCommerce" with the intent to show how the mobile Internet has subverted the entrance to the entire business ecosystem. These new portals value the relationships between people, rather than the function or brand value of a product; the value of social experience lies in the group, rather than personal experience.

In the era of the mobile Internet, when the entrance to the commercial environment places emphasis on human happiness, rather than product value, the product becomes just a carrier of people's true pursuit of happiness, an idea which is the origin of C2B models. In C2B models, customization for consumers is the mainstream of business. Projected C2B consumers exist in tribes, no longer individuals, but people gathered together by common interests, hobbies and values. This model, which I have called "tribal WeCommerce", is based on the logic of human nature in which different groups have the right to enjoy "unique products" that belong primarily to said group, respecting niche markets and individuality. In this sense, the Internet creates a movement of renewed life, in which everyone who joins in is looking for like-minded people with whom to form a new tribe, ridding themselves of the "state" or "companies" in a pursuit of life.

This democratic consumer movement announces the consumer, rather than the business, as the main business body. Business finally has the opportunity to get rid of a "customer-centric" logic of efficiency, and return itself to a "people-centric" logic of life. Tribal WeCommerce companies have made clear that in all human consumption first comes the social significance of a good's consumption, then the spiritual significance of its meaning. One must first "thank God" for a meal, and then use it to live.

More than a hundred years ago, Nietzsche wrote "God is Dead!" to awaken human nature. Today, the mobile Internet has finally returned to human logic, to life itself. In an ecosystem of traditional business, each of us is a "member" of an enterprise. Each customer of a product is "digitized" on a CRM basis. Such a "vertical relationship" is unequal, and no matter how many companies may play God, they are unable to make consumers anything but passive.

By the same token, Taobao is becoming more and more "T-mall-ized", and although not wanting to rebuild an consumer-based business ecosystem like that of Alibaba, due to B2C genes, it will inevitably not be "Taobao", but "T-mall", that is, a large company, on a large scale.

In short, as long as the basic ecology of business foregrounds B2C models, business competition is nothing more than a "marketing war" on business-to-customer relations, attempting to use competing advertizements (in newspapers, magazines, television and now mobile phones) to control consumer time, consumer space, and gain a competitive advantage.

If you are familiar with a bit of corporate strategy theory, then it is easy to understand strategic genius Michael Porter's notion of "five forces": how to compete for all resources and monopolize consumer time (with advertizement) and space (through channels), so as to resist the growth of competitors, the emergence of new entrepreneurs and the establishment of opponents, and this is simply strategy.

Learning how to Perform Tribal WeCommerce in the NBA

We have all heard about the "wolf boy", who, having grown up in the mountains, by age 10 had reached only the IQ of a very young child. This story reflects the fact that the formation and growth of human "selfhood", which includes one's IQ, is created through interactive processes between people. In this vein, the interaction between people is social culture itself.

Here, it is important to emphasize that human interaction is the source of civilization itself. If we look at e-commerce as a new way of life, then life is created by human web interaction. As a group of animals, humans have always lived in an "acquaintance society", in which we say "hello" to acquaintances, nod, make glances, follow rules of social etiquette, and these offline behaviours affect the behaviour of oneself.

Everyone's "self" also contains the social reproduction of "me". In the language of e-commerce, C-C (human interaction) is the most fundamental and decisive social force, creating the social structure and each person within it. The reason that the "wolf boy" had a lagging IQ was due to social lack, a lack of interpersonal interaction, not due to material shortages.

Yes, in the era of the mobile Internet, consumption is no longer simply consumption, but a formative process of a new "netizen" ego. It is precisely this interpersonal interaction on the network that creates a new lifestyle, subverting the industry to bring the vertical relationship of "business-client" to a "customer-client" level, a change which requires business to adapt to a completely new organizational form.

At this point, the tribal ecology of the United States NBA (National Basketball Association) may be said to be ahead of the times: the NBA is a life, and then a business; the NBA is formed of fan interest and hobbies, it is a lifestyle. The team exists and sustains precisely due to the interest of fans, and thus as the business grows bigger and bigger, the product line grows longer and longer.

The Los Angeles Lakers were the first team to be stationed in frigid Minneapolis. As you may know, the state of Minnesota in the United States is "the land of Lake Wanaka", and the team name came from this geographical feature, which would gain the attention of locals. Utah Jazz also chose its name to identify with local residents, as New Orleans is the world's most famous jazz city, the birthplace of world jazz master Louis Armstrong.

It can be said that the NBA is a tribal business model, as NBA fans guide the business, and the business expands with the growth of the fan tribe. Major team decisions, including the addition or removal of players, are not only dependent on player performance, but also on fan preferences.

For example, in April 1987, the NBA decided to initiate teams in four cities: Charlotte, Miami, Orlando and Minnesota. New bosses of these teams invariably announced that out of "respect for public opinion", the naming rights of the teams would go to the fans, holding a ballot vote for each team.

In Charlotte, fans overturned the first team name proposal of "Spirit", and instead chose the name "Hornets". In Miami, where it is hot all year round, residents chose the name "Heat". Orlando is the home of the first Disney World, the reason behind the fan's choice of "Magic". Minnesota chose the "Timberwolves", because, besides Alaska, it is home to the most timberwolves in the United States.

From the very beginning, the NBA's business has been a tribal game in which fans participate in "product customization" and "rule making" processes. When the NBA was founded, there were just thirteen rules in competitive basketball. Now, the NBA Union is focused on the fan's clear understanding of rules, and thereby rules are added to and adjusted annually in accordance with audience views, considering any suggestion that benefits fan participation, even using rules based in other sporting events.

In contrast, FIBA (the International Basketball Association) adjusts their rules only every four years. While FIBA sees itself as a judge, the reason that the NBA is wonderful, is because the league and team managers regard themselves as part of the tribes that serve the teams.

Over nearly sixty years of development, NBA rules have now been extended to a total of 13 chapters, with hundreds of details. There is only one true purpose of these rules, which is to make the NBA more exciting, more fun and more commercially viable; these competitive rules are not absolutes but a product design.

For example, the NBA is a closed league without promotion. Under normal circumstances, commercial investment tends to support championship teams, so championship teams gain more and more money, and the game becomes one of money.

How can a poor team develop without money? Is there an opportunity to "revive a salted fish"? As an answer to this, the NBA introduced two concepts: the "salary cap" and the "luxury tax". Take the 2012–2013 season as an example, in which the salary cap was set at 58 million USD, with a luxury tax of 70.3 million USD. In this case, a team's total salary "hat" was 58 million dollars, and when the total amount reached 70.3 million, the introduction of foreign aid would impose a luxury tax, or even a fine.

Tribal WeCommerce is actually the ecology of the NBA, which I believe stands as the future of mobile business, with a joyful and happy individual at the starting point of the game, putting C (consumer) before B (business), and beginning a business revolution.

CHAPTER 7

FOUR STEPS OF TRIBAL ORGANIZATION

The biggest difference between tribal WeChannel e-commerce and traditional e-commerce is the management of people rather than products. If management is focused around people, we need to find the methods to form tribes. Below, I propose four steps to manage a tribe, describing how to establish an initial relationship among strangers, how to make this weak relationship strong, and finally how to form integrated tribal processes.

The four chief steps are:

1. Entertainment activities: use entertainment to form initial relationships

2. Product experience: use consistency to form strong relationships
3. Trouble-shooting: deal with conflict and locate core partnerships in the formation of self-organizing WeOrganizations
4. Time consumption: use crowdfunding, crowd sharing and crowdsourcing to achieve tribal integration

Initial Relationships: Entertainment Creates Relationships

Entertainment is the best way to make friends, as happiness is a common pursuit of all people, based on instinctive experience. Almost all Internet-based companies rely more and more on game projects to make a profit, highlighting the entertainment value to consumption.

Entertainment is formative at the beginning of relationships, turning strangers into acquaintances. Children begin friendships first of all by playing games, while sports are also very commonly used to bring people together. Familiarity among colleagues within a company is also often established through entertainment activities.

How are Chinese people most likely to spend leisure time? In my experience, most people choose to play mahjong. Returning to my hometown of Guizhou to visit my relatives, the streets are always full of people playing mahjong. When I asked them how many people in the town would come out to play mahjong, they answered that basically everyone did up to the age of 80, but almost no one in their 20s.

Mahjong has become an important way for townspeople to socialize, and it has the benefit of naturally imposing a topic for discussion around the table. I do not know of people who sit around a mahjong table and say nothing, and in playing mahjong you will soon get to know those around you. Playing mahjong helps to form intimate relationships.

Taking mahjong as an example, I would like to illustrate that behind the entertainment aspect of mahjong lies the implication of a crucial "interpersonal relationship" forming. Playing mahjong brings people happiness, and happiness makes us forget our troubles. Therefore, in attracting people to participate in activities that bring happy experiences, such a game poses an important step in turning "strangers" into "relations".

Entertainment is also a social behaviour that imposes certain restrictions on participants. For example, with mahjong, people generally play with a few specific partners, which encourages a deeper pleasure as a result of established interpersonal relationships.

Here, I would like to emphasize two major attributes of entertainment:

Firstly, the natural nature of entertainment: entertainment naturally stems from natural human needs, and therefore one's participation in entertainment, or lack thereof, is determined by instinctual human happiness genes.

Secondly, the social attributes of entertainment: continuous or deep happiness created by entertainment is premised on the establishment of interpersonal relationships, and whether playing, singing, or traveling, "with whom to play" is a prerequisite. Many young people do not want parents or the elderly to join in with their activities, an indication that happiness has very real social attributes.

Knowing the rules of entertaining allows us to grasp one of the most important entrances to the combination of commerce and Internet life: participation in entertainment is the natural starting point of activity, and the social attributes of entertainment suppose access to marketing (trust is marketing).

Hence, we can see that after the Internet takes over the basic ecology of people's lives, people express a value for life (entertainment) before business.

Another important aspect of entertainment activities is that in this game, everyone plays a role and must abide by the rules of the game. Compliance with the rules is a prerequisite for participation; in other words, if a person learns to comply with the rules, he is "socialized". Participation and obedience are precisely what is necessary in a group. If entertainment is the best way to turn "strangers" into "relations", we must also make it clear that social relations based on entertainment form only weak relationships.

WeChat deleted its "aircraft crash" game, as it was able to attract many people, but weakened people's relationships. In other words, upon establishing a weak relationship through entertainment, do not overdo it, as continued entertainment can make even strong relationships weaker, a poor regression.

From Weak to Strong: Active Experience Creates Cultural Experience

Today is an era that emphasizes experience, the importance of experience being its position as a system of perception. Each individual's sensory perception includes several of the same elements: vision, hearing, smell, taste and touch. These are the ways in which we experience the world, and without them we would have no perceptivity.

Actually, the mobile Internet has realized the expansion of this system of perception. Visual experience, for example, was, in the past, limited. Now, with the help of the mobile Internet, we can see all over the world in an instant through mobile phones.

Since the mobile Internet has begun to expand our system of perception, we have found that what we saw in the past was stored in our brains, while what we see now is stored as a system of knowledge through images and videos that may be revived through Weibo and WeChat. What is the difference between online and face-to-face education? Recorded audio lessons may be repeated again and again whilst doing things, and may be shared with friends. This turns the perception system into a system of knowledge.

Such an elevation of human perception to a knowledge system is the biggest breakthrough of the mobile Internet; "mobile phones have become an extension of the human central nervous system". Mobile phone communications extend our vision, our hearing and even our sense of touch.

In this sense, the mobile Internet not only expands our sensory system, but helps people store perceptions in the form of a knowledge system. Once experiences are stored, there is a whole new mode of aggregation in this system — the aggregation of knowledge. In other words, this system of knowledge involves sharing information over the mobile Internet, in a different way to face-to-face education or communication systems. Face-to-face education or communication is limited to certain numbers of people, but with mobile interactivity, we can expand this field of interaction. All communications are stored as a knowledge system, to which people can listen repeatedly, experiencing content with a richness that changes human relationships.

We are entering an era in which "experience is King", and the reason that experience is so important is because of the feelings it can spread, the way it can become "knowledge" as it is ingrained in images and text. Such is the new system of knowledge, premised on the idea that customers are both consumers of products and creators of product ideas and knowledge. This process of creation engenders new social relationships, in a self-organizing form that I call "WeOrganization".

Conflict Gives Rise to the WeOrganization

The transition from a strong relationship to a WeOrganization is facilitated by two forces: the first being integration, like-mindedness and collaboration; the other being conflict, which brings about qualitative relationship changes. In life, we often see situations in which two well connected individuals end up in conflict, like two loved ones who are sweet in the beginning, but are changed by the deepening of the relationship.

The deeper the love, the more frequent the quarrels. Why is this? To answer this, we must review the sociology of conflict. In sociological research, conflict often has positive motivations, as people deal with potential problems in hostile or oppositional ways. For example, in a love conflict, when two individuals in a couple do not wish to break up, one may ask the question: what does the other really mean to me?

Here, we can think about the Cold War, and see that although both parties appeared contradictory in their sentiments, their continued accusations of one another plunged each into self-examination. By both reflecting on themselves, the relationship between sides is transformed substantially, even potentially deepened. The reason for this is that those engaged in conflict cannot be separated from each other; the struggle is based on the necessary relationship between two parties, otherwise they would simply part ways.

Self-organization, or WeOrganization, involves conflict every day. In a conflict, people are divided into "us" and "them" camps, and everyone must make choices to determine which side they will take. This is the mechanism behind WeOrganizations.

The same is true for nation-states, as only in the presence of hostile countries will people's feelings of "patriotism" be stimulated. The precondition for the existence of nation-states is worldwide confrontation. This also explains why Hitler provoked clashes between other nations in WWII, arousing his people's loyal "patriotism".

Creating sides of "us" and "them" is the most exciting element of tribal WeCommerce, inciting people's passion, as commercial competition is no longer a competition of commodities themselves, but how to find one's own kind and destination.

So what exactly is self-organization? As with entertainment, whether voluntarily or subconsciously, we act in a self-organizing way spontaneously. Like with old friends, you need not tell each other how to cooperate, you already know how to deal with each other. There is no need to tell one another what to do, as everyone is responsible for themselves, and that is self-organization.

My conclusion here is that conflict makes conscious use of oppositional events as an important self-organizing mechanism. This mechanism divides people into "us" and "them", ultimately creating self-organized boundaries. Creating clear boundaries allows people to know who you are, what you advocate and what you oppose.

A tribe must have borders, and this is a driving force of cultural creation. If there were no borders, the tribe is insignificant. Of course, boundaries also premise a symbolic system, in which minority groups form their own costumes, language and totems, all within a unique culture.

It is hard to imagine, for example, a team without its own jersey. A jersey is a "symbol" of the emotional connections between fans and the team's identity, and when you wear a team's jersey in a full stadium you will find the world divided in two parts: the "us" also wearing your team's jersey, and the "them" without.

Consumer Crowdsourcing: the Era of Makers is Coming

The advent of WeOrganizations creates a special ecology of crowdsourcing. Tribes incite life, and life has generated demand, and this demand that leads to custom products or customized services is based on the spontaneous participation of consumers.

Over the past ten years, people around the world have engaged in an unprecedented social behavior: people get together and work together to get things done, even those that cannot do the job themselves; this used to be the work of an employee in a firm in a particular field. To put it simply, "crowdsourcing is a form of social production".

So, who is involved in this crowdsourcing revolution? Here are some examples:

Amazon: The online retailer has launched Mechanical Turk, a crowdsourcing Internet marketplace providing crowd sourcing services, with enterprises outsourcing work for a matter of dollars and cents, with individuals getting small payments for completing work.

Peugeot: The Peugeot Design Competition has motivated people to design their own dream car, with the 2005 model designed by a 23-year-old Portuguese student.

IKEA Home: In the "Genius Design" Competition, customers are offered a 2,500 euro reward for the winning design on a multimedia home program, and their work will also be put into production and onto the market.

Tate Britain: This museum possesses huge numbers of artworks dated 1500–2000 AD, and has allowed visitors to write their own explanations for the exhibits. Selected interpretations will be displayed as labels beside the artwork.

This is the creation of a new supply chain in the Internet age, and what we call "crowd creation" or "crowdsourcing". Consumers are no longer simply consumers; they are also creators of products, paid selflessly by the investment in interests, hobbies or self-fulfilment.

This kind of "mass effect" on consumption has even spawned a new term – "maker". The term refers to the process of product creation, during which consumers actively participate and even stand as leaders in creation.

The advent of an era of Makerhood indicates that when consumers have a dual role of customer and maker, the creation of value in business is changed. Such a change may be revolutionary, with the user standing at the head of the supply chain, personally involved in product development and design, rather than just a consumer.

In the era of Makerhood, a "participatory pre-sale order" system has been formed gradually. With clothing, for example, consumers are involved in design and production: product samples come out, are tested by consumers, commented on, then then finalized and produced. You may ask, what does one do if they need a product immediately? The answer is simple. If you are thirsty, drink immediately. In this circumstance, you may choose a "standardized" product like Coca-Cola, or if you are hungry you may eat a fast food product from McDonald's.

The word "consumer" itself comes colored by standardization. Every act of purchasing and using standardized goods is a consumer behavior, in which the product is created as a "standard" rather than based directly on consumer need.

If you are opposed to being a consumer, and want to be your own boss, you must choose a business in what you love; you must be personally involved. Put forward your preferences, add your opinion and pay the fees; this is the cycle of a customized pre-sale system.

In the era of the mobile Internet, the forseeable trend is O2O, in which the line between company and consumer will disappear. Consumption is no longer a simple passive act, but a part of the production line, part of a company's business strategy, and a company does not only operate a system of production, but also a system of consumer consumption.

Likewise, consumers not only consume products but also the production process. Here, we treat everything from raw materials to finished products as part of the production process. Consumers will use the mobile Internet to have deep involvement in this process.

An era of consumer-company integration is coming, and the borders between the company and the user are disintegrating.

CHAPTER 8

THE LOGIC OF SPEED IN TRIBE FORMATIONS

n the era of mobile Internet, we are entering a society of speed. In this society, everything is changing rapidly, and it may be called "fast society". Speed has become a competitive advantage for three reasons:

First, "fast" implies the future, and in the face of speed people are looking toward the future, rather than at the present.

Second, "fast" offers a chance to correct mistakes, which is known as "iteration" in the age of the Internet.

Third, "fast" means an accelerating towards the future, representing the forthcoming realization of a future in which "a beautiful event is imminent".

The formative mechanisms of "fast society" lie in the mobile Internet's preoccupation with the mobile phone. In just a small screen, what more could the mobile phone offer? It is "fast', "simple", "instantaneous", creating an "integrated" world of hardware, software and services; this is "fast consumption".

The logic of "fast consumption" is based on entertainment or gamification, and the creation of all products is starting to rely on "entertainment or gaming", almost an inevitable trend. But "fast society" also has a price, in the form of people's "low sense of security". Speed means that we often face an unknown "darkness", so how can we reduce our sense of fear?

The answer: if others are around you, you will not be afraid; a group of people provide one another with a sense of security. This conclusion is important in mobile e-commerce because it reveals that the way humans deal with uncertainties and fears of the future is not, in general, through pieces of scientific knowledge, but through the motivations of "tribal reasoning".

Tribal WeCommerce has become the mainstream of mobile commerce, and its mystery is here. When people associate with one another, and when people feel emotional support, they find their fear of the future falling away from the depths of their heart, and they are able to walk forward with confidence – a unique phenomenon of human psychology.

So, contrary to the logic of "fast consumption", tribal logic is "slow". "Fast" logic is attached to activity, and acting quickly;

"slow" logic speaks to life, and "living slowly", and as such "fast" and "slow" assume different missions. "Fast" takes on a goal of scientific and technological innovation, while "slow" involves the pursuit of humanistic concerns.

The real value of a tribe is largely manifested in the system of tribal symbolism, that is, the need for members of a tribe to use only a few symbols to convey and understand meanings, and thus to feel happy in experiencing belonging. The process of creating such symbols may be "fast", but they are implicated in a "slow" progression.

As an example, friends often have what people call "knowing smiles", with which they acknowledge each others' meanings, while outsiders remain on the outside of this friendship symbolism.

This symbol may be relayed "fast", but it takes time to gain meaning, to slowly experience and gauge such feelings. In this sense, the Internet has created a rapid convergence between people, but it will take time to form "symbols" of such aggregation.

When first seeing a person, we generally make judgements based on their physical appearance. A second symbol may be clothing, and everyone spends energy selecting the clothes with which to express themselves. The saying "people rely on clothes as horses do on saddles" indicates that in the instance of social contact, we are made by our chosen clothing.

The third indication of an individual's personality is their headgear. In ancient China, there was a ritual, in which a man would tie his hair in a bun and wear a hat to demonstrate his entrance into adulthood. In the "Book of Rites" there is a saying: "a twenty-year-old man is a hat and a name". In the same way, in different national cultures, various hairstyles indicate a woman's age and characterize her social status.

The fourth symbol of a person is their accessories, such as watches, bracelets or rings. In social activities, beyond an attention to clothing, people also wear rings, earrings, necklaces, brooches etc in correspondence with specific occasions.

The fifth symbol is action. Physical gestures, or "body language", for example, are a form of interpersonal communication. Different kinds of body language may represent different things in different cultures, and one's circle of friends may use special "internal body languages" to communicate differently with those inside the circle as opposed to outsiders.

The result of human interaction is actually a "symbol", meaning that the process of forming "tribes" involves the creation of "symbols" that people commonly recognize, and this takes time. Moments are fast, but human life is slow; this is certain.

Creating Cultural Symbols, Forming Tribal Brands

If we were to compare the cultural symbols of the United States and China, we can pick up a lot of inspiration.

For example, some of the main cultural symbols in the United States are Wall Street, Broadway, Hollywood, McDonald's, the NBA, Coca-Cola, the Hilton, the Statue of Liberty, Barbie, Football, Jazz, Starbucks, Wal-Mart, etc.

In China, symbols include Beijing's Forbidden City, the Great Wall, Suzhou Gardens, Confucius, Taoism, the Art of War, Terra Cotta Warriors, Mogao Grottoes, the Tang Empire, Silk, Porcelain, Peking Opera, the Shaolin Temple, Kung Fu, the Journey to the West, the Temple of Heaven, Chairman Mao, Acupuncture, all 20 forms of Chinese cooking, etc.

Side by side, we can see that American culture is largely representative of modern business culture, whilst Chinese culture is filled with historical symbols. We in China also appreciate Wall Street, Broadway, Hollywood, McDonald's, the NBA, Coca-Cola, Disney, Starbucks, Wal-Mart, and this is "Westernization". Americans enjoy the Forbidden City, the Great Wall, Suzhou Gardens, Confucius, the Terra Cotta Warriors, the Mogao Grottoes, the Tang Empire, silk, porcelain, the Beijing Opera and Shaolin Temples.

These examples demonstrate that there is a "tribal recognition" behind "cultural symbols". Tribes of interest created through the Internet have become more "niche", and compared with "mass" symbols, the time it takes to produce niche cultural symbols is greatly shortened. When the real asset of a tribe is its symbols, they must be formed "slowly", and here "slow" has two implications: one being that the core value of a tribe is minimal, and two that the creation of cultural symbolic systems involve a process of elimination and refinement. This process is "unapologetic", and must be carried out "slowly".

Another layer of meaning comes in the "miniaturization" of the mobile Internet, which makes cultural symbols more diversified, transcending the boundaries between countries and regions, as well as the traditional system of cultural symbolism. Such is the creation of what are known as "bit cloud assets".

Building a "bit cloud asset" is a "slow" process, in which what is changed is the environment, and not people's sentiments. The mobile Internet is in the business of human beings; this is commerce for people, and it is worth considering the following four points:

1. The value system of human society is actually represented by symbols to a large extent. The symbolic system represents cultural accumulation, while also representing the values of human communication.

2. The real value of a tribe is not its assets, but the unique symbols it creates, that is, a set of symbols commonly recognized by people.

3. Cultural logic is "slow". The process to create a valuable symbol system of one tribe should not be "fast", but must proceed "slowly".

4. Stories are sometimes necessary in order to carry and circulate the symbols to an end of intergenerational transmission.

CHAPTER 9

NO MORE TALK ABOUT THE COMPANY - LET'S TALK ABOUT THE WEORGANIZATION

The reason why tribes are different to the company is that the company is an organization, while the tribe is self-organized. Organizations rely on rules and data for management, while self-organization relies on "alternative values". What does "alternative values" mean here? It means that tribal WeOrganizations put value in the future, attending to feelings, values and morals, rather than emphasizing institutional norms and control as corporations and governments do.

As we all know, the initial development of human society existed in tribal forms. Basic survival modes of tribes are based in blood relations, that is, tribal families are made up of webs of family ties. In such tribes, people associate with one another based on blood or affection. Why are those within such tribal structures so honest? Because the cost of betrayal in this kind of environment is very high, and without a tribe one has no way to survive.

From the roots of tribal bloodlines, with clan-based, moral, customary management, we have moved to organized systems of standard social management, and this is a great sign of human progress. However, in today's Internet age, human beings have returned to the tribe, with mobile phones allowing people to re-aggregate and reform a new era of "tribal survival".

The Impetus of the WeOrganization: A Leader's Courageous Persona

French existentialist Jean-Paul Sartre famously said "hell is other people", revealing a very important phenomenon: in the period of the industrial revolution, human life was characterized by alienation, loneliness and helplessness. Industrialization and urbanization moved people out of tribal living arrangements, and they entered "professional" life. Humans began to aggregate for work rather than personal affection, and what a miserable situation it was.

Indeed, urban life in industrial society brought revolutionary change to human living standards. People needed much more time to get to know and trust a person, perhaps not speaking a single word to a neighbor in the course of years.

Today mobile e-commerce has reinvigorated "tribes", these "tribes" reviving traditional "acquaintance logic" in which business is premised on a "warm tribe". As in ancient tribes, people are committed to the creation of trust, bonding over common goals and creating symbols, a process which is begun, first and foremost, by a leader.

WeOrganizations may be spontaneous, but there is always an initial impetus, and this trigger is in the form of a leader. Leadership stands for the core of "personalized values", and without such a leader, interactions would be scattered randomly. In different real-life occasions, we can observe this sense of leadership: one who always "sacrifices themselves for everyone else".

From the perspective of interactive theory, when leaders create benefits for everyone, beneficiaries respond in following the leader or accepting their leadership, opening up an opportunity for WeOrganization formation. In fact, organizations or groups will forever endure formative costs, and most people are motivated to join groups if they can attain a benefit provided by the organization, but who exactly provides these benefits?

Initially, most instances of self-organization were initiated by leaders who, through interactions, identified like-minded followers and then took a stance in times of conflict, prompting self-organization to achieve norms and discipline. For example, in a "group" on the Internet, in order to create a "favorable" environment, stopping random advertizements and disruptive conversation, leaders formulated rules and discussed these rules with a group of like-minded followers, initiating offline gatherings and "crowding out" non-group members in the environment.

New roles emerged as members appearing to be disorderly or unorganized slowly merged into "unilateral" pathways via the interactions between leaders and followers. This "unilateral nature" represents the beginning of differentiation amongst people's social roles, as we consciously or subconsciously grasped tribal values.

Why do people appreciate such restraint? Because people are a group of animals, and the only prerequisite for happiness is the tribal idea of "unilateral groups of people" – those who have the same values and similar interests, and such formations create the greatest happiness.

In Maslow's heirarchy of needs, in addition to physiological needs, humans demand certain features of identity. Approval from a group provides a sense of security, and only after a person has their own identity may they form a foundation of socialization, with the possibility of being respected, and without identity life has no meaning.

This effect allows leaders to gain "legitimacy" in leadership and power. In other words, the technological ecology created by the mobile Internet is itself an "ecology of character", more in line with human happiness than technicality.

Small Logic: From a Focus on Objects to a Focus on People

When we go shopping, there is always a similar experience: endless browsing before selecting a product, hesitation over the real or potential defects of various products. The more we look, the less we know what we want. However, once we purchase a product, the shop in which we buy it gains value in our minds, even disregarding others' negative opinions of its products.

Such an experience can be attributed to a psychological linearity: once you possess something, the relationship between yourself and the object is changed, and the quality of the item is no longer as important, because it represents your own judgement, and everyone instinctively supports their own judgement.

Yes, this is what is called the "small logic" of social psychology: no matter what kind of product is selected, the quality of a product is a matter of one's own judgement. People look for a variety of reasons to support their choices.

The Internet system is a people-focused ecosystem, and the ecology of mobile commerce providers is based on the premise of similar people with similar interests converging. In an environment of human aggregation and social exchange, the small logic of social psychology has a crucial role. Based on this theory, the relationship between things and human beings becomes "self-conceptual", transforming the process of role recognition between people.

More specifically, small logic is a starting point for free or experiential models. In this instance, free by no means indicates something is "easy to consume", but something beyond the exchange of benefit. In addressing free or experiential models as cheap, one not only underestimates consumers, but, more importantly, this view will lead to the deterioration of consumer ecology.

Small logic emphasizes that in the Internet age, the exchange of products and customers is no longer simply about economic exchange, but is a social exchange that is rich in social content, indicating an overall development of tribal micro-commerce business that has nothing to do with the size of a company, and the relationship between customers and products exists on a different frequency.

This is very important. It means that even a few dozen or so people in a tribe can operate a business because of human involvement rather than a product. Dozens of people can form a life group. At this point, it should be clear that the process of managing people is no longer the logic of products, but a psychological process of a group that is based on small logic.

As long as small logic is established, it instigates a new business model, and through the small logic of small products, new participants with the same interests will be found to create a tribal identity. Is what we call "venture capital" not the investment in this new consumer ecology? If the correct consumer ecology can grow quickly on its own, what is the significance of venture capitalism?

Based on this, tribal WeChannel e-commerce is an entrance: beginning from a tiny place, making small products into big products. Since tribal lifestyle involves the aggregation of interests, hobbies and values, tribal WeChannel e-commerce involves the operation of a "style" of small products as realized through shared values.

From the beginning, I have suggested that the logic of mobile e-commerce is that "life is greater than business", and there is a focus on people as people rather than just customers. Now we can see more clearly that the key to opening up business and life is to start with small logic, and use small items or services as carriers to form large user bases, clarifying the boundaries of "us" and "them" through participation.

Social anthropologists, in the study of primitive tribes in Africa, have found that many tribes have similar customs, that is, in the instance of a festival, people often exchange gifts in the form of small bracelets, necklaces or other such trinkets. Researchers have found that through the exchange of these small gifts, inter-tribal interpersonal relationships were able to be maintained and even sublimated.

As a result of studies like this, we have a deeper understanding of the unique features of mobile commerce, in which one is not operating a product, but a user. From a human point of view, rather than a business point of view as in the transaction of goods, the core entranceway to mobile e-commerce is a shift in focus from product competition to human competition; the real focus is people, not things.

CHAPTER 10

WECHANNEL E-COMMERCE: FROM CONSUMER TO CONSUMPTION MERCHANT

From a sociological perspective, humans have been through three transformations in modern times: the first was the transfer from a time of "God" to secular society, known as the "Renaissance Era". Secular life as such was the origin of modern culture. Second was the transfer from government to enterprise, in the era of the "market economy", in which enterprises propelled the industrial revolution. Third is the transfer from organization to individual, the "age of mass data", in which the individual takes the leading role in information network society.

At present, we are in a revolutionary process of the third transformation, in which the individual is becoming the main force behind four "We's": WeMedia replacing media, WeChannels replacing traditional channels, WeBrand replacing classic branding and WeOrganization taking the place of established organizations. The substitution of WeMedia has already taken place, that is, the individual has already taken a primary position in media, shaking the status of traditional media outlets and circulation. As such, the power transfer in regards to media is almost complete.

Now, we are going through the second phase, in which channels dominated by individuals are rising, known as "WeChannel e-commerce micro-leadership". What is micro-leadership? I define it as: consumers are upgraded to the status of consumption merchants, as past of a new channel dominated by individuals using WeMedia concepts. The upgrade of consumers to consumption merchants is the essence of the "WeChannel", and the biggest difference between micro-leadership and e-commerce is that e-commerce is primarily focused on B2C models, while micro-leadership is about C2C interaction. E-commerce remains dominated by enterprises, while WeChannel e-commerce is dominated by self-organizing individuals. E-commerce has replaced the retail channels of enterprises, while WeChannel e-commerce is overhauling the whole selling channel of enterprises, as well as their internal marketing systems.

Uber is actually a derivative, in which part-time drivers are defined as "micro entrepreneurs", with a motto that "everyone can be a micro entrepreneur", taking advantage of unexploited resources by pioneering a "start up" for talent. But in this case, WeChannel e-commerce runs much deeper than Uber, and Uber is just an example of micro-business regarding "the optimization of talent".

My conclusion here is that WeChannel e-commerce has made important breakthroughs on the basis of talent in such Uber-type models. Just imagine what more could be shared, taking Uber as a basic example of the Sharing Economy. In essence, Uber requires a car, and the driver becomes an appendage of said car. As such, you must possess a car before becoming an Uber driver. This is Uber's first limitation threshold, sharing objects rather than people.

Uber's second limitation is that no matter how excellent a person might be, for example, a consultancy management expert like me, he or she can only become the driver of Uber if he or she wants to join Uber, which undoubtedly limits the participants. However, Uber has the potential to completely open up its management system. Experts like me, for example, could earn money by becoming part-time management trainers for Uber driver groups. Etiquette professionals, too, could become part-time trainers for Uber drivers to improve drivers' professional levels, and so on.

As such, WeChannel e-commerce offers important

breakthroughs in these two areas: it is not based on sharing objects. While Uber first requires people to have a car to share skills and services, WeChannel e-commerce is in the business of human sharing. Only the spirit of entrepreneurship is required, and with the help of a cell phone you can join in the sharing economy, earning money by offering users products and services over mobile networks. I call this "Uber-like talent", and we can see what business miracles are possible with the sharing of talent as compared to Uber's car sharing model.

With a basis in sharing people, enterprises can open up a huge number of positions within the organizational system, sharing excellent social talent that will not only save enterprise administration expenses, but stand as an important breakthrough to traditional enterprise management. An enterprise's administrative, marketing, HR and even financial positions can be assumed part-time by users with relevant talent, as such skills are no more only required by enterprises, but by society at large.

That is to say, the essence of WeChannel e-commerce is not just about "business", but it is more importantly about the innovation of the structural organization systems. WeChannel e-commerce teams will replace the organizational teams of enterprises, and the prevailing enterprise formation of the last one or two hundred years will be transformed; that is the emphasis of WeChannel innovation.

In short, mobile e-commerce will be more powerful than PC e-commerce. If PC e-commerce companies such as Amazon, Alibaba, T-mall and Taobao have changed the traditional retail system, WeChannel e-commerce will not only change the retail system, but also the enterprise's organization and brand interpretation, ultimately changing the whole business ecology to form a completely new "DT business ecology".

Four phases of Mobile E-commerce Development Between 2014 and 2024

In the next ten years, mobile e-commerce will develop quickly, rapidly replacing PC e-commerce models. The changes in these ten years may be summarized as such:

- We, the readers and authors, will become WeMedia, thoroughly changing the transmission pattern (already completed)
- Consumers become WeChannel micro leaders, changing the business pattern (in progress)
- Individuals operate their own organizations, changing the management pattern
- "Friend circles" becomes WeBrands, changing the business lifestyle

The first phase (2014)—WeMedia completely triumphs: from Facebook, Twitter and Instagram to Chinese micro blogs, WeChat and so on, a global transformation has been completed, leaving the mark of rising "social media". Information publication has been transferred to social media bases on mobile phones, shifting from TV, newspaper and magazine channels.

The second phase (2014–2018)—the rise of WeChannel micro leaders: in this phase, every consumer has the right and capacity to post information due to the maturity of WeMedia. The enterprise's monopoly on "flow traffic" is blocked, with every consumer able to make sales through individual channels, now known as "WeChannel e-commerce" in China.

Just as taobao.com, a subsidiary of Alibaba, was implicated in controversy due to counterfeit goods ten years ago, WeChannel e-commerce has also now been trapped in criticisms of "pyramid schemes". However, WeChannel e-commerce is inevitably destined to become symbolic in Chinese mobile e-commerce, just like T-Mall and Taobao have been.

Why will WeChannel e-commerce inevitably become the mainstream channel in the future of mobile e-commerce? The answer to this can be understood by comparing WeMedia and traditional media. What is the difference between traditional media and WeMedia? If the function of traditional media is the penetration of information from top to bottom, then the function of WeMedia is to publicly display information from bottom to top. In this way, the biggest difference between channels and WeChannels is that a channel functions to sell from top to bottom, while WeChannels function to garner participation and "crowd source" from the bottom to the top.

The third phase (2018–2021)—people become brands. This is a period when users create consumer brands as individuals, a period of tribal culture. In this moment, WeMedia and WeChannels will be mature, and people will become their own brands for their own products.

The so-called people's brand has two aspects: first is trust, given that people no longer trust the brands of big business; second is cultural symbolism, that is, users will be a part of the product value chain and cultural creation process, in which the brand is no longer established by centralized companies but self-organized tribes.

The fourth phase (2011–2024)—the rise of C2B models focusing on "WeOrganization": in this period, WeMedia, WeChannel and WeBrand will be mature, and the key problem will be how to establish a system in which users operate, manage and develop by themselves, without a channel system dominated by enterprises.

In 2016 in China, the total sales amount of WeChannel e-commerce was 360 billion RMB, and is expected to reach two trillion or so in the next three years of rapid development. There are two main characteristics in Chinese WeChannel e-commerce:

first, using people rather than stores (traditional models), or network platforms (online store models such as Taobao, JD, etc.), as channels for commerce; second, business activities are carried out by social media platforms (WeChat).

In an Internet environment of transparency, the product itself is unlikely to entice "high premiums". On the contrary, platforms such as Amazon and Alibaba will inevitably drive enterprises to engage in "price battles". When WeChannel e-commerce uses social media as a carrier, business comes from a new starting point. Social platforms first create trust and "interactive value", meaning that values of communication and identification between people presuppose business.

In the future, I believe agencies will disappear, but the services from products to users will increase. The value of WeChannel e-commerce is the achievement of premium brands via avenues of creativity and service. How does WeChannel e-commerce create such a premium brand? It forms clients into tribes, and realizes customization and/or personalization of products. Niche tribe "WeBrands" will thus replace standardized brands.

Tribal WeChannel E-commerce: the "Tribe + Partner + Angel Distribution" Trinity Model

If Amazon, Taobao and T-mall have shaken the traditional channel system, the tribal WeChannel e-commerce focusing on social e-commerce sways the enterprise's internal organization system.

This can be seen in the replacement of traditional e-commerce systems with WeChannel e-commerce. Tribal WeChannel e-commerce has two main parts: the first is that operating partners replace traditional wholesalers, and, once strong, eventually the

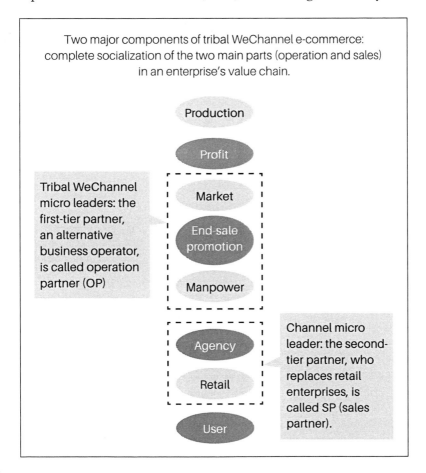

Two major components of tribal WeChannel e-commerce: complete socialization of the two main parts (operation and sales) in an enterprise's value chain.

Production

Profit

Tribal WeChannel micro leaders: the first-tier partner, an alternative business operator, is called operation partner (OP)

Market

End-sale promotion

Manpower

Agency

Retail

Channel micro leader: the second-tier partner, who replaces retail enterprises, is called SP (sales partner).

User

marketing and advertising departments. Second is angel agents, who replace traditional retailers.

The second step is self-organization within a WeChannel. Then, a tribe creates crowd content, in a similar fashion to basic "crowd-sourcing" as described on Wikipedia. A product in the crowd-sourcing or crowd-creating system, which is characterized by niches and personalization, is imbued with diversity and life, a huge contrast to the standardization, modeling and scaling of traditional industry.

Now, let us look at these two parts separately.

Partners are not only tribal operators, but also product wholesalers and/or group purchasers — the value of wholesale or group buying is, to a large extent, the reduction of logistics costs, beneficial to profitable operation in regional markets. The partner system has two values:

First, services to Angel Agents, similar to "crowdsourcing". WeChannel e-commerce operates on a logic of singular categorization, meaning that one group manages only one product category. The advantage of this is that WeChannel e-commerce teams are each gathered around one singular product category, proceeding with direct "crowd-sourcing" or "crowd-innovation" in which each WeChannel micro leader is the "prospective expert" of the product.

The second value of partners is in setting up a regional O2O service system in order to establish a regional O2O market and regional gathering location based on wholesale levels (for example, large-scale procurement). Without a localized partner's wholesale model, C-based O2O cannot be established, which is why most current O2Os are struggling to succeed.

Tribal WeChannel e-commerce is based on angel agents. An angel agent is labelled as such because the core of retail is to be "social" rather than "transactional", and the most value provided to a user is in the form of interactive value, i.e the exchanges between people, (communication), in sharp contrast to the function value emphasized in the product era, and the band value provided by the service era.

Here, it is clear to see that tribal WeChannel e-commerce is a system based entirely on service to establish a heirarchy. "Angel agents" are actually consumers themselves, that is, the WeChannel, just as in WeMedia in which users became the media. So what is a partner? Partners are not "merchants" but organizers and operators who serve "angel agents". Their roles are most likely separate from manufacturers, acting as third-party service agents.

CHAPTER 11

NEW 4P MODE: FROM THE OPERATION OF PRODUCTS TO THE OPERATION OF PEOPLE

When mobile e-commerce upgrades the B2C sales mode to the humanistic "tribal C2C mode", or even the C2B mode, does this also mean that the popular 4P model of marketing that has existed for decades (product, price, place, promotion), will withdraw at this historical juncture?

Yes, people-focused, rather than customer-focused, requires us to reconstruct the meaning of 4P marketing, and in this context we must redefine the 4P model in terms of mobile e-commerce:

First of all, the first P in the traditional 4P scheme is product. In the mobile Internet era, what is sold is no longer simply a product, but a service and culture of people.

Secondly, in the past, products needed to find the right price in order to penetrate the market, while now all a product needs is passionate fans.

Thirdly, products once needed a place to be sold. Consumers in new 4P times are the selling locale, the channels — WeChannels, the partners of enterprises and dealers.

Fourth, promotion is no longer one-way, but involves the full participation of users.

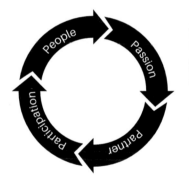

Traditional 4P	New 4P
Product	People
Price	Passion
Place	Partner
Promotion	Participation

From product to people, price to passion, place to partner, promotion to participation, I feel the transformation from the old 4P to a new 4P represents the entrance of business into a brand new era called tribal WeChannel e-commerce.

Tribal WeChannel e-commerce does not only sell products, but also sells services and culture to people in a tribal system from the point of view of people. Culture needs passion, and when passion enters the WeChannel, partnerships are made between enterprises and passionate fans. At this point, promotion is no more sales from one side to another, but the comprehensive participation of passionate fans.

From this point on, the sales system structure is completely changed, no longer emphasizing how to compete in prices, but how to foster fans in a human way. It is no longer bidding for a selling location, instead searching for partners with similar interests with which to build bonds and share the benefits. There are no more promotional exaggerations, but voluntary participation and clear communication across the network.

Next, I would like to share a new 4P marketing case that I participated in myself.

New 4P case: Calling the Icewine "Sleeping Beauty"

By chance, at a party once, I tasted some icewine produced in the Meili snow mountains in China. In my mind, rare, famous and expensive icewine was usually produced in cold places like Canada and Germany. Frankly, I enjoyed this icewine mostly because I was shocked by its place of origin. Meili is the name of a place near the Diqing region of Tibet, and the famous Meili snow mountain is among what is known in Tibetan as the "Kawagarbo snow-capped mountains", a range with the average altitude of over 6000 meters. The main peak is forbidden for climbing as a holy site of the "Yong Zhong Rulai Buddhist Doctrine" (the oldest Buddhist doctrine in Tibet). What precious wine, produced in such a holy place.

Later on, I discovered that the vineyard where the icewine is produced is arduously kept by the local Tibetan people. The Tibetan religious belief absolutely forbids the spraying of pesticide and fertilizer in the vineyard in such a holy place, so as to keep full pureness of the holy land. I grew to really appreciate this wine, and formed a tribe with my friends who also like it. We decided to place an order with the manufacturer for the wine.

I intend to explain the starting point of the new 4P marketing theory by narrating this story: in today's rich life of the mobile Internet, the momentum of users in WeChannel e-commerce comes not from making money, but from the enjoyment or love of life itself. It is a new life that consumers create, rather than just a business.

Our wine tribe is based in a WeChat group. We often chat in the group, discussing things such as how to give a personable name to the product, how to make the product more "human" as well as exclusive among our group. We also discuss the contradictory phenomenon of red wine culture, in which Westerners like to drink wine at arbitrary moments, while Chinese people mostly drink wine at dinner time, while entertaining guests or at a festival celebration. We then decided to try out this Western way of life, and the first things we did when we got home was drink a small glass of wine. When chatting with family members, we also tried chatting and drinking. A small glass of wine half an hour before bed every night can help sleeping, and as time went on, we had certain special feelings. Every time we would lift up the cup to slowly drink a glass, the sweet fruit aroma unique to the icewine was refreshing, a feeling like the meeting of old friends who have not seen one another in a long time.

Thus, we more readily understood why Chinese people generally drink mostly when entertaining guests or celebrating a festival, both typical examples of social consumption. The amusement factor of wine is present when drinking whilst communicating with relatives and friends, and the joy does not lie in the wine itself. "When drinking with close friends, one thousand glasses of wine are too few". Happiness comes from close friends rather than wine itself, which also explains why Chinese people prefer to drink liquor, as liquor has a higher alcohol percentage, and is therefore more relaxing and more stimulating to those reserved from opening their minds.

As previously mentioned, wine culture originating from the West is different from liquor culture in China. In the scheme of Maslow's hierarchy of needs, people who drink red wine are mainly pursuing "self-realization", while drinking liquor is the pursuit of social integration. Why do fewer and fewer Chinese people drink liquor? Perhaps this indicates that Chinese people are walking towards "self-realization" from "social belonging", as seen by their wine consumption.

We finally called Meili icewine "Sleeping Beauty", and this was largely propelled by the females in the tribe. Those who are familiar with Grimm's Fairy Tales may remember that Sleeping Beauty was asleep for a long time, and eventually wakes up. As a branding symbol, Sleeping Beauty intends to speak to females in an Internet era who are shaking off the devil's curses and marching towards "the revival of human nature".

Hence, we complete the first P of the new 4P marketing mode, that is, to transform marketing from product marketing that relies on function to cultural production. From a cultural outlook, we may turn and look at the second P: passion. What is passion? Strictly speaking, I think the Chinese meaning of passion cannot be expressed clearly in English. In English, the original meaning of a passionate person is a zealot, a lover.

The "Sleeping Beauty" tribe has held many activities, gathering many fans through its own media production. Of course, one indispensable thing at its fingertips is a personified brand spokesman, the "first impetus" of cultural creation and communication. "Sleeping Beauty" rates a "New Queen" every month, and an "Annual Queen" at the end of each year, and those who excel naturally become tribe partners, paying for the tribe to reap its benefits.

Our "Sleeping Beauty" tribe does not put out sales promotion, but holds social activities in which the right people will gather and communicate happily with other consumers. Remember the sentiments of Sam Walton, the founder of Wal-Mart: many believe that Wal-Mart became rich overnight, but those people are unaware that there were twenty years of hard work before that moment. Such an idea clarifies the core of new 4P marketing, as well as C2B business. C2B plays in the reputation economy, belonging to the people, and it stands a chance of developing faster if it is operated slowly.

CHAPTER 12

CORRELATION: THE NEW PHILOSOPHY OF MOBILE E-COMMERCE

One day, I was watching TV and the screen showed an American astronaut landing on Mars. At this time, my daughter wanted to watch cartoons, and when I asked her to wait, she worriedly asked me, "Daddy, why do you care about Mars? What do we have to do with Mars?"

I was dumbfounded instantly by this question: she was right, what do I have to do with Mars? This question has puzzled me for a long time since, and it has made me question other things I see. Later, something accidental gave me an answer, but also triggered my thinking about the Internet.

One winter evening two years ago, I drove home after working overtime. When I was about to drive into my garage, I saw a person pushing a cart peddling apples. Normally, I would have driven directly into my garage, but that day I felt pity; maybe I could sense his trembling cold and the eagerness in his eyes. I knew he would be wishing I would buy some fruit, so I stopped my car and walked toward him. When I was picking fruit, I received a call from my daughter. She said she wanted some fruit to eat, and asked if I could bring some back. Just in that moment, I felt an extreme shock inside my heart, because a minute ago I had been there just out of sympathy, to help a fruit peddler who I could not stand seeing endure the freezing cold wind.

Just a minute later was my daughter's call, and I wanted to thank the fruit seller. I knew that had he not been near my home, I would have had to go out of my way to buy fruit, and if I didn't, and went home with nothing, I would feel guilty in the face of my child. At that time, just because of this fruit seller outside my house, I was easily able to buy fruit and received a simple opportunity to be a good father. Ever since then, I often think of this experience and my quick change of heart.

I started to ponder exactly what factors and situations would cause us to ignore certain things like the fruit seller. When we look for ourselves, we may notice that there are certain people right at our door who can provide us with happiness.

By the same token, convenience stores, hairdressers, laundries and other service systems at the forefront of the community are automatically ignored when we do not need them, and one day, when we do need them, we find ourselves full of gratitude. Such services silently accompany us, just like the man selling fruit in the cold of winter.

In learning about mass data theory, I realized that it is essentially a principle of relativity regarding Internet data. Relativity here is to say that the world is actually a huge system, and there is an inherent relationship between all the world's things, but each of us will only pay attention to the things that are of use to them, those which are valuable, and we respond to everything around us with such causal logic.

The danger in this causality is that we will only focus on things that are useful, that can directly benefit us, and participate in things that seem to be worthwhile and beneficial. As a result of this logic, when we do not buy fruit, we ignore those selling it around us, only paying attention to them when we need the product. We forget a simple principle of relativity: a happy life cannot be separated from a good ecology of service, and the service ecology abides by relevant logic — what is useless right now, will not necessarily be useless to you in time; and is not necessarily useless to others.

Pragmatism is the Natural Enemy of Mobile E-commerce

The danger in "causal logic" lies in the fact that is has destroyed the organic connection between lives, or destroyed the internal connection of the world. Once we separate the original connections between lives and the world, the source of innovative ideas is extinguished, and human souls become pragmatic factories commissioned by each of us.

Consequently, we begin to think only vertically between "useful and useless", becoming completely oblivious to the accidental connections between man and all things (horizontal thinking).

On the one hand, the Internet is greatly significant in the restoration of connections between people and things. The world has always been an organic ecosystem, and there are essential links among people as well as with people and things. With the Internet, whether you are in Beijing or New York, in the mountains or at the seaside, people are connected through mobile phones, able to truly to realize the dream of a "global village".

Such is the mindset of the Internet: human life encompasses the whole world; the whole is human, and humans are the whole. Internet thinking means that in regards to things, we are able to connect with any person and/or thing we think of in the formation of a valuable whole.

Because of the Internet and the Weibo, WeChat and BBS (electronic bulletin board) systems that operate within it, we have broken "causal" boundaries, and "fruit stalls" join us and become a part of us.

The starting point of all of this is "correlative thinking", we no longer ask whether a thing is of use to us, but what a thing correlates to. According to the theory of the "six degrees of separation", any two people need only a maximum of six intermediaries to establish contact, and people, through certain contacts, inevitably produce correlative relationships.

This means that any two people are actually "related" in a way, but without the Internet, the cost of such "relativity" was so high that we believed only a few people in the whole world were connected to us, and the world became a "causal world".

Only in understanding the Internet from the perspective of relativity and understanding e-commerce can we truly understand the significance of this revolutionary, new era. Internet thinking, first of all, is a theory of connection between people. If we can recognize that the chief feature of the Internet is the breakdown of limitations in time and space, then we must also break down the corresponding world outlook and methodology that accompanies such limitations.

Everyone confronts two worlds: one is the physical, a "living causal world". In this world, I am only attuned to those directly related to me, useful to me, such as loved ones, such as buying fruit; think of the stalls.

There is also another world, the virtual world on the Internet, a correlative world in which everything is connected. In a correlative world, we care about everything that is "related". As created by the mobile Internet, this world moves you, me, him and "them" all together. You and I are no longer just human beings, but we both exist in a cosmic network; no longer a global village, but a network village.

Two manifestations of correlation must here be emphasized once more: First, the value of diversity — what has no value for you does not necessarily have no value to others; Second, the value of space-time — what has no value for you now, will not necessarily have no value in the future.

These two manifestations of relevance are very important, as they redefine the existence of value: value is no longer an inevitability, but a contingency, a result of chance. As such, value is no longer just practical, but also creative.

The difference between correlative thinking and causal thinking is that correlative relevance requires that we no longer only study internal mechanisms in events, but pay more attention to the phenomenon of "direct correlation". Just the same as when, on the way home, I suddenly discovered the correlation between fruit stall owners and the well-being of our lives.

In knowing this, we no longer simply equate happiness with the causal chain of "existing and being useful", but seek to find facts and figures that are relevant to our well-being in our living environment. Facts and figures allow us to discover new possibilities, which can create happiness directly.

In other words, we need to pay more attention to the possibilities of existence, not simply explore "internal inevitability".

From the eyes of God, this so-called causal logic of human beings is a reciprocal logic invented by people in a small space. Correlation, however, is a "logic of possibility" in an open world. This logic of possibility frees people from "linear thinking" or "vertical thinking". Instead of sticking to mechanistic analyses and causal assumptions, a logic of possibility searches directly for people or things to create new possibilities.

I believe that this is innovation.